Time Out
for
Prayer

Julie Baker

Cook Communications

Cook Communications Ministries, Colorado Springs, Colorado 80918
Cook Communications, Paris, Ontario
Kingsway Communications, Eastbourne, England

TIME OUT FOR PRAYER
©2000 by Julie Baker. All rights reserved.

Printed in Singapore

1 2 3 4 5 6 7 8 9 10 Printing/Year 04 03 02 01 00

Editor: Glenda Schlahta
Cover Design: Jeff Lane
Interior Design: Pat Miller

The Library of Congress Cataloging-in-Publication Data
Baker, Julie, 1955-
   Time out for prayer / Julie Baker.
     p.cm.
   ISBN 0-78143-409-2
    1. Prayer—Christianity. 2. Christian women—Religious life. I.
Title.

BV215 B34 2000
248.3'2—dc21   99-087511

Contents

Dedication

*To my incredible family and loving friends
who stand in the gap for me.
Ezekial 22:30*

Introduction

Years ago, there was a popular television show called *Magnum, PI*, starring Tom Selleck. In one episode, Magnum is stranded at sea, clinging to a small piece of wreckage from his blown-to-bits boat. Treading water, he prays, "O God, if You save me from this, I promise never to lie again or play pranks on Rick." A few hours later the stakes get a little higher: "O God, if You save me from this, I will sell my sports car and give the money to the island orphanage." His final plea just before rescue: "O God, if You save me from this, I'll sell everything I have and become a priest!"

Needless to say, the next week's episode finds him driving his sports car, fudging on the truth, and certainly playing pranks on his sidekick, Rick.

In your life, does prayer boil down to being just a bargain you make with God in moments of desperation, something you practice when there is nothing left to do and no place else to turn? God does indeed want to be our help in times of trouble, but He intends prayer to be much more than that.

This book is designed to lead you in experiencing what prayer is all about. Each section addresses a different aspect of prayer. Read the introduction to set the tone and for an overview. Then over the next weeks, read and meditate on the devotionals in that section. Every devotional follows the same pattern: God's Word as the starting place, brief thoughts about the topic and Scripture, a brief sentence to help you begin your own prayer, and a place to record your reflections about what you've read, what you want to say to God, or what He is saying to you.

At the end of each section, use the Action Steps to reflect back over the devotions of the past days and what God is teaching you.

If you want to know our Father in a new and more intimate way, read on. Your life will never be the same!

Introduction
Why We Pray

~~

W hat brings you to your knees? Do you pray out of desperation to a God that you don't really feel you know? Do you pray mainly for things you want, hoping that God will grant your wish? Do you pray looking for advice? Maybe you pray wanting a closer relationship with your Heavenly Father.

God hears us when we pray, no matter why we pray. But true prayer is more than just asking, even for good things. True prayer is change—not necessarily of our circumstances, but of ourselves. As Richard J. Foster says, "In prayer, real prayer, we begin to think God's thoughts after Him: to desire the things He desires, to love the things He loves. Progressively we are taught to see things from His point of view."[1]

We can lay anything at the foot of the cross . . . but the real point of laying it there is to align ourselves with the perspective of God, in the matter of the moment and in all things.

Why do we pray? For many reasons. But why can we pray, and what are some things we *can* pray about? Let's open the Scriptures and see.

The Resting Place

Jesus is the resting place
I look into His loving face
He shelters me from harm this day
And shows His mighty way
In the storm He whispers, "Peace be still"
And I yearn to know the Father's will
Soon the troubled waters disappear . . .
He takes away my fear

Jesus is the resting place
A solace from life's hectic pace
He holds me in His mighty hand
And tells me whose I am
In the storm He whispers, "Peace be still"
And I keep my eyes on Him until
I'm safely through the troubled sea
And from my burden freed.

Chorus

"Come unto me, you weary ones and lay your burden on the
    Son
Take my yoke and learn my gentle heart
The peace I give will not depart
And I will give you rest."[2]

We Pray Because He Hears

*"This is the confidence we have in approaching God:
that if we ask anything according to his will, he hears us."*
(1 John 5:14)

*H*e hears us. Aren't those beautiful words?

We spend our lives with people who want *us* to hear *them*. Children, husbands, parents, coworkers . . . they all need things from us. And for the most part, we're happy to give—but isn't it nice, for a change, to know that there is a place where we can be heard? Where Someone actually wants to hear what we say?

We've all had those conversations with people who appear to be listening, but aren't really hearing a word we're saying. They nod, maybe say, "Mmmm," occasionally—but their minds are elsewhere. And let's admit it. We've spent a few conversations doing it ourselves. All too often we are more interested in the thing we're planning to say next than in hearing the other person. Or even more insulting, our mind may be wandering to what we're going to fix for supper or what errands we need to run.

God isn't that way. And He'd like us not to be that way when in conversation with Him! Did you catch the stipulation in the verse? *"If we ask anything according to His will."* How can we know His will? By *listening* to Him—to His Word as we read; to His voice as we pray. The closer the relationship we develop with Him, the clearer His voice will become.

Thank You, Father, for truly listening, not only to what I say, but also to what You see in my heart. Help me to seek Your will as I pray and trust You for the answers. . . .

My Thoughts

We Pray Because He Forgives

"If he has sinned, he will be forgiven."
(James 5:15)

Mark 2 records the touching story of a paralyzed man whose friends wanted Jesus to heal him. They carried him on a pallet to the house where Jesus was teaching, but the place was too crowded for them to even get near the door.

Undaunted, the friends found another way. Maneuvering the pallet onto the roof, they dug a hole and lowered the man in front of Jesus as He was speaking. Undoubtedly, the crowd was shocked at this interruption, but not Jesus. Instead, He was impressed with their tenacity and creativity. And He was touched by their faith.

Obviously, Jesus knew the reason for their persistence; they wanted their friend physically healed. Yet the first thing that Jesus said to the man was not, "Stand up and walk," but, "Son, your sins are forgiven" (v. 5).

What?! The man had come to Jesus so he could walk. What did sin have to do with it?

Sin had—and has—everything to do with it. Even if we are healed of our physical ailments, it's still only a matter of time before we get sick again and, eventually, die. But if we receive a spiritual healing—if our sins are forgiven—we've received an eternal healing that guarantees us everlasting life.

There's a lesson for us in this story. When we come before God, we need to set aside our physical, temporal concerns and focus first on our spiritual condition. Are there sins we need to confess? Have we taken time for praise and fellowship with the Savior, or are we rushing on to our list of wants and needs?

Lord, help me to be aware of the spiritual realm that stretches so far beyond this temporal one we live in. Let me prioritize my life and my prayers accordingly. . . .

My Thoughts

We Pray Because We're Dependent on Him

"Let the little children come to me, and do not hinder them, for the kingdom of heaven belongs to such as these."
(Matt. 19:14)

I can still remember impatiently awaiting the birth of our daughter. Even more clearly, I remember holding her for the first time, aware of the awesome responsibility of caring for this totally helpless little being.

Little children are completely dependent upon their parents. They need us to provide food, clothing, shelter, love—everything they need for survival. We spiritual children aren't much different, except that we fool ourselves into thinking we're able to attain anything at all on our own. As James says, "Do not be deceived . . . every good thing bestowed and every perfect gift is from above, coming down from the Father of lights" (1:16-17, NASB).

When we pray, it reflects our dependence upon God. It reminds us and it assures Him that we understand that everything we eat, all of our clothes, our place of lodging, and each breath we take is dependent upon His mercy and provision.

After all, when Jesus said, "for the kingdom of heaven belongs to such as these," He was telling us that heaven belongs to the meek and needy . . . those who humbly admit their need for a Savior.

Lord, help me remember that all that I am, all that I have comes from You. Keep me from pride and help me to humbly acknowledge Your gracious gifts. . . .

My Thoughts

We Pray Because God Is Our Help in Times of Trouble

"Is any one of you in trouble? He should pray."
(James 5:13)

*I*f there is one experience common to everyone in the world, it is trouble. It may be of our own making; it may be from situations beyond our control. But whatever the source, the answer is the same: *pray.*

In fact, prayer is one of the benefits of being in trouble.

Benefits? That's right. James tells us to be thankful for our trials, and a revved-up prayer life may be one of the reasons. After all, troubles definitely tend to make our prayer life more abundant, and more time spent with God leads to a greater understanding of His character. Knowing God's character gives us the faith that He is with us in all our troubles, and that gives us peace. Not only that, but *having* a need keeps us dependent upon God for *meeting* all of our needs. And bringing our needs urgently before God makes us all the more aware of how He answers our pleas, giving greater confidence in the future when we bring our requests before Him.

No wonder James began his book with the words, "Consider it pure joy, my brothers, whenever you face trials of many kinds" (1:2).

Lord, remind me that if I never had a need, I'd never see You meet it. . . .

My Thoughts

We Pray Because It Is the Only Thing That Works

"This kind can come out only by prayer."
(Mark 9:29)

Mark 9:14-29 recounts the poignant story of a boy possessed by an evil spirit. In desperation, his father brings the boy to the disciples in hopes of seeing him delivered from this torment . . . but, try as they might, the disciples have no success. This must have confused them greatly; they had been healing and performing miracles on a regular basis up to this time!

When Jesus approaches, the crowd rushes to meet Him, babbling anxiously about what is happening. Jesus addresses the father and gets the story, imparting a different lesson altogether to this doubting dad. Then He commands the spirit to come out of the boy, and it does.

Later, the disciples ask why they had not been able to cast out the demon. And Jesus replies, "This kind will come out only by prayer." Apparently, the one thing the disciples had not tried!

Even when we are gifted in certain areas, even when we serve the Savior every day, we still need to be aware of our need to pray. Sometimes, it's the only thing that works.

Lord, help me never to forget, in the busyness of my day, in the

tasks I do for You and others, that the most important thing on my list is prayer. . . .

My Thoughts

We Pray Because We Want Wisdom

"For the Lord gives wisdom, and from his mouth
come knowledge and understanding."
(Prov. 2:6)

*S*olomon, billed as the wisest man to ever live, was appointed by his father, David, to rule over Israel at the tender age of twenty. In a dream one night soon afterward, God appeared to Solomon and offered to give him whatever he asked (1 Kings 3:5).

What would you have requested—wealth, long life, ten more wishes? Solomon asked for a discerning heart with which to govern God's people.

The Lord was so pleased with Solomon's request that He gave him not only what he asked, but many things for which he did not ask: "both riches and honor, so that there will not be any among the kings like you all your days" (v. 13, NASB).

James tells us, "If any of you lacks wisdom, let him ask of God, who gives to all men generously and without reproach, and it will be given to him" (1:5, NASB). God's wisdom is as available to us as it was to Solomon, and it pleases Him when we seek it.

Lord, I, too, am but a child who does not know how to go out or come in. Grant me wisdom in all I do, that I might serve You better. . . .

My Thoughts

We Pray Because We Need Comfort

"Praise be to the God and Father of our Lord Jesus Christ, the Father of compassion and the God of all comfort, who comforts us in all our troubles, so that we can comfort those in any trouble with the comfort we ourselves have received from God."
(2 Cor. 1:3-4)

The Greek word for *comfort* in this passage is *paraklesis*, which literally means "calling to one's side." According to *Vine's Expository Dictionary*, it combines encouragement with the alleviation of grief.[3]

Are there times when you need to have someone by your side? When you need encouragement? Alleviation of grief? Of course there are. It may be because you've lost a loved one; it may be because you've lost a job, parted with a friend, moved to a new place, or just have any empty ache inside that won't go away.

How fortunate we are to know the "God of all comfort" (2 Cor. 1:3). What a relief to know we are not alone! Whether He meets our needs through His own loving presence, or whether He brings people into our lives to be His kind face and His embracing arms, He will not leave us to suffer by ourselves.

Father, thank You for filling me with Your comfort when I feel alone or abandoned. Help me to be aware of others to whom I might bring the blessing of Your presence. . . .

My Thoughts

We Pray Because We Want to Know God's Ways

"If you are pleased with me, teach me your ways so I may know you and continue to find favor with you."
(Ex. 33:13)

When Moses spoke these words, he was full of exasperation—and fully aware of his need for the Lord. He was doing his best to lead the Israelites into the Promised Land, but they were shooting themselves in the foot at every turn. No sooner had he returned from Mount Sinai with the Ten Commandments than he discovered the people dancing and singing in worship of a golden calf. Furious, Moses threw the stone tablets down, and they shattered. And now he was having to ask for a new set—but even more important, he was begging for the Lord's presence.

Have you ever been frustrated with the behavior of those you are in charge of? Your children, maybe? Or the people you work with? Perhaps a Sunday School class full of third graders? Then you can relate to Moses. And what's more, the Lord can relate to you. Even He was put out with the Israelites. In fact, His very words to them were, "Should I go up in your midst for one moment, I would destroy you" (v. 5, NASB).

It is both a privilege and a pain to be responsible for others. Sometimes we handle it well; other times, we are at our wits' end. Don't wait until you reach that point to call out to God.

Ask Him to teach you His ways now! It is only through knowing Him that we can know how to lead.

Aren't we fortunate that God's Word can be written on something more substantial than mere stone tablets; it can be inscribed on our hearts.

Lord, without You, I can only wander in the wilderness with those I lead trailing along behind me. Teach me Your ways so that I can lead these people to You. . . .

My Thoughts

We Pray Because We Need Rest

"Come to me, all you who are weary and burdened, and I will give you rest. Take my yoke upon you and learn from me, for I am gentle and humble in heart, and you will find rest for your souls. For my yoke is easy and my burden is light."
(Matt. 11:28-30)

How many times have your burdens in life seemed as though they were too heavy to carry?

So often, we hear people say, "God never gives us more than we can bear." But it isn't true! Quite frequently, our loads in life are more than we can handle—alone, that is. In fact, sometimes I suspect He lets our loads get a little too heavy just so we'll realize how inadequate we really are.

What a beautiful invitation Jesus gives for those of us who are weary and burdened. He doesn't necessarily want to help us escape from the burden. Rather, He wants to take the load from us so that we can rest.

An old-timer once explained to me how you train a team of oxen to plow a field. The first thing you need is a yoke. That yoke is designed to fit around the neck of not one, but two oxen, and it forces them to pull the plow together, at the same speed, side by side. Usually, this man said, you pair a young ox with a veteran ox that knows the lay of the land and the commands of the master. When they are yoked together, it is the older ox that is actually shouldering the entire burden while the younger one merely walks alongside.

How often do we shoulder our way into the yoke of the older ox, trying to pull the whole load ourselves? Jesus wants us to shift our burdens onto His back, letting Him bear the weight, while we merely walk alongside Him, learning how to plow our fields.

Lord, my load is too heavy for me to bear alone, and I don't know the lay of this land. Please take my burden so I can rest and learn from You. . . .

My Thoughts

Action Steps

We are propelled toward God because we desire answers to our prayers, fulfillment of our needs, and comfort for our weary souls. Think through and list specific attributes you would like to obtain in your journey of spiritual growth.

List specific areas where you would like to receive wisdom:

_____

_____

_____

_____

_____

_____

List needs you have to be fulfilled:

_____

_____

_____

_____

_____

List areas where you are seeking God's comfort:

_____

_____

_____

_____

_____

List the names of those you are praying for:

_____

_____

_____

_____

_____

_____

_____

List areas where you need to seek God's forgiveness:

_____

_____

_____

_____

_____

_____

Now spend a few moments reviewing the list and bringing each need to the Lord. Begin by praising Him and thanking Him for who He is, and end by thanking Him for the prayers He will answer.

Section 2

Introduction
Preparing for Prayer

*P*rayer is a resource as constantly available to us as a twenty-four-hour hotline. Our Father who loves us is always available, always listening, always ready with a reply. There's no such thing as a busy signal or call-waiting when it comes to reaching God!

Some of us may not have quite begun to believe that yet. For some, it seems unbelievable that the Lord of All waits to hear their voice—and so their voice in prayer comes out timid and unsure, and they are hesitant to come into His presence.

Others of us, however, are quite used to the idea that God hears our prayers. For us, prayer seems about as captivating as milk gulped down on our way out the door. It's important; we always keep it on hand; in fact, we make frequent use of it. We just don't give it a lot of thought or preparation, any more than we make a big event out of pouring and drinking that glass of morning milk. For us, prayer has become too casual—and, truth be known, less effective.

There's an important balance to strike between the confidence with which we can approach the throne and the reverence and care with which we ought to approach it. It's not a balance you can find overnight. As Richard Foster says, "One of the liberating experiences in my life came when I understood that prayer involved a learning process. . . . We should remember that God always meets us where we are and slowly moves us along into deeper things."[1]

In this section, we will be looking at some of the attitudes and practices that enhance our prayer life. This is not a list of prerequisites for prayer, any more than holiness is a prerequisite for salvation. Yet neither are these things insignificant. They are things that please God, and that enrich and empower our prayer life. Like little children gaining in maturity and knowledge as they grow, let's take these things into our hearts, seeking to understand and apply them a little more each day.

Open Hands

Lord, we come to You today with an open hand
So that we can give away the things we do not understand
We give to You our bitterness, our pain and failures too
And with this outstretched open hand surrender all to You
Lord, we come to You with an open hand

Lord, before You now we stand with an open hand
So that we might understand the grace and mercy of Your
    plan
Help us receive the fullness of Your love's redeeming pow'r
And let us feel Your presence grow with every passing hour

Lord, we come to You with an open hand

Chorus

Open hands and open hearts, receiving His joy in full—not part

The Savior's waiting with gifts abundant to place within your hands

Open hands and open hearts, letting go as hurts depart

The Savior's waiting to take it all from an open hand

He gives joy and He gives peace

His tender mercies will never cease

The Savior's waiting to place it all in your open hand[2]

Praying in Jesus' Name

"And I will do whatever you ask in my name, so that the
Son may bring glory to the Father. You may ask me
for anything in my name, and I will do it."
(John 14:13-14)

few years ago, we were privileged to host Elizabeth Dole at one of our TimeOut for Women! conferences. I didn't know her personally, but Mrs. Dole is a friend of my TimeOut cofounder, Betsy DeVos.

Betsy had already laid the groundwork for bringing Mrs. Dole into our conference. Still, I was very nervous the first time I called her office at the American Red Cross. The receptionist asked how she could direct my call and I said "to Mrs. Dole." She hesitated and asked about the nature of my call. I simply told her that I was calling in reference to a matter Mrs. Dole had discussed with Betsy. "Oh! I'll put you right through!" was the response.

In much the same way, we gain immediate access to God when we come to Him through the name of Jesus Christ. Of course, God doesn't need to be reminded who we are. But using Jesus' name reminds us of His position as intercessor—the very reason we have access to God at all.

Praying in Jesus' name also reminds us to pray the way Jesus Himself would pray. Are we praying with the attitude of a servant? Are we showing as much concern for others as we are for ourselves? Are our prayers reflecting an eternal perspective rather than an earthly one?

When I talked to Mrs. Dole, I was very careful to be polite, direct, efficient, and friendly. Since I had used Betsy's name to gain access to Mrs. Dole, I wanted to make sure that I represented myself in alignment with Betsy's graciousness. And since Betsy had stuck her neck out for me, I didn't want to let her down!

Jesus did more than just stick out his neck for us. He laid down His life. And through this sacrifice, He gives us direct access to a holy God.

Jesus, thank You for allowing me to use Your name to gain access to the Father! . . .

My Thoughts

Forgiving Others

⇒)⊂=

"And when you stand praying, if you hold anything
against anyone, forgive him, so that your Father
in heaven may forgive you your sins."
(Mark 11:25)

When someone hurts us unfairly and walks away without repenting or apologizing—it hurts! And the hurt festers inside until it becomes bitterness, tainting our thoughts and deeds, making us miserable. There's only one cure for this downward spiral, and that's forgiveness.

Forgiveness, though, is perhaps one of the most misunderstood concepts in the Bible. The misconception is summed up in the phrase we casually toss out when someone accidentally bumps into us, or forgets a lunch date, or breaks a glass—"That's okay."

But forgiveness is not saying, "That's okay." Because unrepented sin is not okay. More accurately, forgiveness is choosing to let someone off the hook of accountability *to us* for their actions—even though what they did was wrong. It's deciding to allow God to deal with that person's wrongdoing, rather than stewing over it and trying to deal with it on our own. After all, as Hebrews 10:30 tells us, vengeance isn't our right. It's His.

Jesus knows how hard forgiveness can be. He Himself performed the greatest act of forgiveness on the cross when He, though sinless, bore the punishment for our sins, paving the way for us to have a relationship with His Father. He put forth the offer

34

of forgiveness; but it was up to us to repent and receive that forgiveness before a right relationship with God could be established.

Likewise, earthly relationships cannot be restored until there is not only the offer of forgiveness, but repentance on the part of the wrongdoer. Mark 11:25 requires us to do only that which lies within our power—release any grudges we might hold and make forgiveness available to those who have sinned against us.

If we don't do that, we ourselves are sinning. And our prayers are not effective if we are harboring sin in our hearts (Ps. 66:18). Forgiving an unrepentant person doesn't do much for that person—but it purifies our hearts and motives so that we can stand in prayer before the Lord and know He will hear us.

Thank You, Lord, for Your forgiveness that You have offered to me at such a great price. Please help me to extend forgiveness to those who have sinned against me and caused me pain. . . .

My Thoughts

Reconciling with Others

"Therefore, if you are offering your gift at the altar and there remember that your brother has something against you, leave your gift there in front of the altar. First go and be reconciled to your brother; then come and offer your gift."
(Matt. 5:23-24)

$\mathcal{F}$orgiving others can be hard . . . but just as hard is asking others to forgive us.

Let's be honest. The sins of others are just far easier to see than our own, aren't they? How often have we inwardly grumbled about our husband's flaws, or self-righteously observed the shortcomings of a friend, while completely disregarding our own? Often, even having become aware of our own misdeeds, we ask forgiveness from God . . . but not from the person we have sinned against.

Asking God's forgiveness for our sins is right and good; it restores our relationship with Him. But the Bible continuously emphasizes the importance of our relationships with others as well: "Be at peace with one another" (Mark 9:50b); "Live in peace with one another" (1 Thess. 5:13b, NASB); "Pursue peace with all men" (Heb. 12:14a, NASB).

So important, it seems, that God is willing to put His own relationship with us on hold until we make things right with others.

Father, make me aware of the wrongs I have done to others,
and give me the courage to admit them and seek forgiveness. . . .

My Thoughts

Becoming Righteous

"The Lord is far from the wicked but he hears
the prayer of the righteous."
(Prov. 15:29)

What exactly is righteousness? According to
Unger's Bible Dictionary, it is "purity of heart . . .
being and doing right."[3]

I don't know about you, but I seldom fully meet that standard. Does that mean that my prayers aren't heard? Fortunately, Christ has made us righteous before God through His death on the cross, and now God's ears are forever open to us.

> God made him who had no sin to be sin for us, so
> that in him we might become the righteousness of
> God (2 Cor. 5:21).

But does that excuse us from behaving as righteously as we are able? Of course not. Philippians 2:12-13 admonishes us to "work out [our] salvation with fear and trembling; for it is God who is at work in [us], both to will and to work for His good pleasure" (NASB). In other words, we are to let the righteousness that has been attributed to us (through the work of Christ) become reality in our lives (through the work of the Holy Spirit).

Living out the righteousness we've been granted has many benefits. Among many other things, it allows us to experience the kingdom of God (Rom. 14:17); it helps us find peace (Heb.

12:11); it earns God's blessing (Prov. 3:33)—and, perhaps most valuable, it imparts effectiveness to our prayers. As James 5:16 tells us, "The effective prayer of a righteous man can accomplish much" (NASB).

Lord, thank You for the righteousness that I have before You because of the Cross. Please help me to attain that same righteousness in my day-to-day life. . . .

My Thoughts

Having Humility

"Do not be afraid, Daniel. Since the first day that you set
your mind to gain understanding and to humble
yourself before your God, your words were heard,
and I have come in response to them."
(Dan. 10:12)

Yesterday, we learned that boldness is a quality valued by God. Today, we see Him responding to humility. Doesn't that seem like a contradiction?

Only if you think of humility as low self-esteem or a sense of unworthiness—considering yourself to be lowly and undeserving. But biblical humility is not defined that way.

Biblical humility is simply recognizing who we are before God—fallible, sinful, but dearly loved. It is free from pride (1 John 2:16). It considers the needs of others (Phil. 2:3). It produces gratitude (Col. 3:17). And, perhaps most importantly, humility focuses on God, not self (Is. 37:16).

One of the most stirring examples of humble prayer is Psalm 8. In it, David recognizes both God's majesty and our position in God's heart:

> O Lord, our Lord,
> How majestic is your name in all the earth! . . .
> When I consider your heavens, the work of your
>   fingers,
> the moon and the stars, which you have set in place,

what is man that you are mindful of him?
And the son of man that you care for him? . . .
You made him a little lower than the heavenly
  beings,
And crowned him with glory and honor (vv. 1, 3-5).

What a privilege it is to be so loved by such a great God.
And what an honor to be allowed into His presence.

*Lord, I thank You for Your interest in me, and for Your desire
to hear my prayers. In the face of this great love and kindness,
help me to remember who You are. . . .*

My Thoughts

Praying with Intensity

"So I turned to the Lord God and pleaded with him in prayer
and petition, in fasting, and in sackcloth and ashes."
(Dan. 9:3)

Daniel was just a teenager when his people were taken
into captivity by the Babylonians. Even though he
was young, and even though he was living among
idolators, he maintained his commitment to God and even grew
in it throughout his life. When he was in his eighties, he realized through reading the scriptures that the time of captivity was
almost over. But his joy was soon replaced with despair as he
realized that the nation of Israel had drifted far from God.
Unless something happened to change them, their release would
only unleash another Babylon into the world.

Grief-stricken, Daniel prayed fervently over the sins of his
people. He literally took on the behavior and dress of those in
mourning, wearing sackcloth, sitting in ashes, and fasting.

And God honored his prayer. Before Daniel even finish his
petition, the angel Gabriel came to him with a message from God.

> "As soon as you began to pray, an answer was given,
> I have come to tell you, for you are highly esteemed.
> Therefore, consider the message and understand the
> vision" (Dan. 9:23).

No doubt part of the reason God answered Daniel's prayer
so quickly was Daniel's consistent faithfulness through the years.

But when our hearts are broken over the things that break God's heart as well, and when our prayers are fervent and in accord with His own desires, it's as if He has been sitting ready to answer, waiting only for us to begin our request. As Matthew 6:8 tells us, "Your Father knows what you need before you ask him."

Oh Lord, let me be fervent in my prayers for the things that move Your heart. Give me passion where Your own passion is strong. . . .

My Thoughts

Becoming Responsive

*"Because your heart was responsive and you humbled yourself
before the Lord . . . and because you tore your robes and
wept in my presence, I have heard you, declares the Lord."*
(2 Kings 22:19)

King Josiah was the sixteenth king of Judah and took
the throne at only eight years of age. Although his
father and many generations of relatives before him
(except Hezekiah) had done evil before the Lord, Josiah was ten-
derhearted toward God and walked in all the ways of his fore-
father, David (2 Kings 22:2). When he was twenty-six, he
ordered that the damaged temple be repaired. In the process,
Hilkiah, the high priest, discovered a copy of the Book of the
Law.

"When the king heard the words of the Book of the Law, he
tore his robes" (v. 11). He was horrified that Judah had strayed
so far from the law of God. Although he was just one king in a
long string of defilers, Josiah chose to break the cycle. His heart
was responsive to God's Word, so God's heart was responsive to
Josiah.

Today our prayers can still break the cycle of godlessness
and sin in our families and cultures. It may take time, but God
honors the prayers of those whose hearts are responsive and
humbled before Him.

Lord, I want to stand for You, whether anyone else does or not. Help me to see your plans and follow Your heart in all that I do. . . .

My Thoughts

Obeying the Commandments

"[We] receive from him anything we ask, because we
obey his commands and do what pleases him."
(1 John 3:22)

This appears to be a blank check, doesn't it? Yet our experience tells us that God does not always give us whatever we ask. All of us can think of things we've pleaded for that we have not received, perhaps things we are longing and praying for even now. So how can we reconcile our experience with this passage?

As always, it's important to read the verse in its context; the surrounding verses shed much light on its meaning. But the prerequisites of our petitions being granted begin right in this verse itself: "because we obey his commands and do what pleases him."

What commands does He mean? The next verses tells us.

> And this is his command: that to believe in the
> name of his Son Jesus Christ, and to love one
> another as he commanded us. Those who obey his
> commands live in him, and he in them. And this is
> how we know that he lives in us: We know it by the
> Spirit he gave us (vv. 23-24).

Sounds pretty simple. We believe in Christ; most of us settled that issue long ago. And love each other—well, we certainly try, don't we? But abide . . . well, that's the tricky one. It's so easy for Christ to get pushed into a back corner of our hearts. Not intentionally, of course, but there's soccer practice, and dinner to prepare, and those committees we serve on. Life just gets in the way.

Yet God acts on our prayers when they are in accordance with His will (1 John 5:14). And how can we pray in accordance with His will if we are not abiding in Him?

For that blank check to be signed, it comes down to just one thing—pursuing God. Being "so immersed in the milieu of the Holy Spirit"[4] that we automatically pray in accordance with His will.

Lord, I want to abide in You, to be immersed in the Holy Spirit. Please help me to seek You out in the midst of my busy, distracting life and learn to please You in all I do. . . .

My Thoughts

Staying Clear Minded and Self-Controlled

*"Therefore be clear minded and self-controlled
so that you can pray."*
(1 Pet. 4:7b)

When was the last time you felt truly clear minded?
Most of us live in a constant state of distraction. But
distractions can reduce the effectiveness of our
prayers, so it's important to minimize them as much as possible.
Here are some strategies that may help:

- Pray at the same time each day.

- Remove anything that will interrupt you—take the phone
  off the hook, turn off the TV, and ignore the doorbell.
  And let your family know that this time is inviolable
  except in a case of emergency!

- Increase your concentration by participating physically in
  your prayers, keeping a journal and checking off each item
  as you pray for it.

- Learn to tune out all thoughts that do not pertain to your
  prayer list.

Why does Peter add self-control to this verse? Perhaps
because it relates so closely to clear mindedness. If we are not
self-controlled, we won't be able to resist that ringing phone or
doorbell. We won't be able to say "wait" to that child's demand

for toast or to the to-do list that keeps intruding on our thoughts. Maybe we won't sit down to pray to begin with!

Like any relationship, our relationship with God takes time and effort, or we lose touch with each other. We schedule dates with friends and spouses; let's be just as deliberate about communicating with God.

Lord, I want to spend time in prayer with You. Help me to make prayer a priority in my life, and keep me from giving in to the distractions that keep me from it. . . .

My Thoughts

Fasting

"Even now," declares the Lord, "return to me with all your heart, with fasting and weeping and mourning."
(Joel 2:12)

asting means going without food or water so that time normally spent eating can be spent with God. It gives us an opportunity to abandon the physical to embrace the spiritual. God instituted the Day of Atonement, or day of fasting, as one of the laws given to Moses. Obviously, it was a day set aside for confession, repentance, and forgiveness of sin.

With the coming of Christ, we were freed from the law. In the New Testament, there is really no commandment given by God requiring us to fast, but there are times when it is suggested that we do so—mostly for what it does in us. In Acts 13:2 we read that the apostles, while fasting, learned of the Holy Spirit's instructions to "set apart for me Barnabas and Saul for the work to which I have called them." Then in Acts 14:23 fasting is mentioned again: "Paul and Barnabas appointed elders for them in each church and, with prayer and fasting, committed them to the Lord, in whom they had put their trust." The early church received much insight, instruction, and direction from the Lord through the apostles' prayer and fasting.

When we are in the midst of making serious and life-changing decisions, fasting helps us to focus on the issue and allows God to see that we are doing our part in committing the circumstance to Him. My sweet husband will often leave the house at

6:30 A.M. to spend time at his office before work in prayer. Rather than sleeping later and eating, he chooses to let God know that his priority is to gather wisdom for the day. He has often received profound insight during these times of fasting.

Fasting must be a private exercise with God. If we fast only so we can boast of it to others, we have defeated our purpose. If, however, fasting allows us to concentrate in a sacrificial way and devote extra time in prayer, God will surely honor our efforts.

Lord, I hunger only for You. Please fill me with Your Spirit and direct my thoughts as I pray. . . .

My Thoughts

Action Steps

Our prayers are most effective when the condition of our heart is right. We've discovered some practices that can help our hearts become more in tune with God. Review this section and choose one or two areas in which you struggle. What are they? Why are they difficult for you?

_____

_____

_____

Are there some habits you could develop that would make your prayer life more consistent and distraction free? List those things here.

_____

_____

_____

And remember: God loves you and longs to spend time with you. Bask in the presence of the Lord and just soak Him in!

SECTION 3

Introduction
How to Pray

$\mathcal{P}$rayer is an act so simple that a small child can do it. It is also so complex that it has baffled scholars for centuries. The questions are numerous, and no doubt you've asked many of them yourself: Do our prayers really change anything? Why do we need to pray if God already knows what's in our minds? Why does God sometimes seem so silent in response?

We may never know all the answers. But one thing we do know is that prayer is a vital part of our relationship with God. And while the Bible doesn't spell out one right way to pray, it is replete with examples and even instructions that help us form some ideas of how to go about it.

In this section, we'll visit some of the instructive passages and eavesdrop on some of the prayers found in Scripture. And as we go, we'll try out some of the principles we discover.

But remember—no matter how you pray, no matter where, God is waiting to hear your voice.

Up to the Mountain

As the crowds pressed in to see this man from Galilee
They saw a man of peace shrouded in humility
And they wondered at His calm authority
Where did He find the strength they all could see?

Chorus

Then He went up to the mountain to pray
He went to the Father in the heat of the day
And there by faith He received great strength
To minister and show us God's way
He was tempted and tried
He was beaten, denied
Yet He gave not into sin
He has asked us to live in the power He'll give
As we love and worship Him

In the heat of the hour when you're battered and scarred
Follow Jesus' footsteps to the mountainside afar
For to those who wait on Him He'll give great pow'r
He'll give needed strength to face each trying hour[1]

Take Time to Pray

⮞⮜

*"After he had dismissed them, he went up on a mountainside by
himself to pray. When evening came, he was there alone . . ."*
(Matt. 14:23)

*A*fter he had dismissed them . . . by himself . . . he was
there alone. Don't you like that? Aren't there times
when you want to dismiss the people in your life, to
go off by yourself, to be alone? There's not a thing wrong with
that feeling.

On this particular day, Jesus must have felt especially emptied
and in need of replenishment. Earlier in the day, He had gotten
word of John's beheading. His first instinct was to take off in a boat
and be alone, but "the multitudes . . . followed Him" (Matt. 14:13,
NASB). Sick at heart, He was still moved by their needs, and He
spent the day healing them, well into the evening. Finally, His disciples suggested sending them away so that everyone could eat,
and so that they could close up shop for the day. But Jesus would-
n't hear of it, and next came the event every Sunday School child
can retell—the feeding of the five thousand (not counting women
and children) with the five loaves of bread and two fish.

And then finally, the leftovers were gathered, and the people went away, full both physically and spiritually. And Jesus
collapsed in a heap on the sofa and . . .

No. Jesus sent His disciples away, and He went to do what
He'd wanted to do all day—spend some time with His Father.

Maybe we're not healing the sick and feeding the multitudes, but our days can get pretty full too. Sometimes we, too, have to put off what we really need to do—go off by ourselves and pray. But, like Jesus, we need to make sure it eventually happens. There is no end to the demands on our time; if we leave it up to our families and friends and communities and churches, there will never be a window of time in which to sit down and be with our Father. At some point, we need to send everyone away, go up to the mountain, and pray.

Lord, please help me not to get so wrapped up in my daily responsibilities that I fail to lean on You for strength, wisdom, and rest. Nudge me off to the mountain where I can hear Your voice and be nourished. . . .

My Thoughts

Without Ceasing

"Pray continually."
(1 Thess. 5:17)

*I*s it possible to actually perform an action without stopping? Well, we breathe without stopping. We blink continually. We swallow without even thinking about it. These are such natural functions that we do them continually without effort or thought.

It may not be feasible to spend our entire life on our knees praying, but we certainly can adopt an attitude of prayer that does not stop.

When I come to the point where I am so dependent upon God that I turn to Him in every situation on every occasion, I must, out of necessity, turn to Him constantly in prayer. As I recognize that He lives within me, I claim the power that He instills in my spirit to make right decisions and take refuge in His loving arms. Out of my heart of gratitude and joy flows the desire to obey Him.

The verses on either side of this passage encourage us to "be joyful always," and "give thanks in all circumstances." God doesn't request that we be happy about all our circumstances. Life is tough sometimes, with challenges way beyond our own grasp. However, when we pray without ceasing, we have the inner enthusiasm from God to be thankful not *for* the circumstance but *in* it.

Oh, that our life of prayer was so constant that it was as natural to us as breathing, swallowing, and blinking!

Lord, with each breath I take, I yield my life to You. . . .

My Thoughts

Submit to God's Will

"Yet not as I will, but as you will."
(Matt. 26:39)

*J*esus may have preferred praying on mountainsides, but He spent what must have been His most intense night of prayer in a garden. At least, it was called a garden. But it wasn't full of flowers and winding paths; it was full, instead, of giant stones and troughs used for pressing the oil out of olives. It was not a place of relaxation, but of work—most appropriate, since in just a few short hours, Christ's most important work on earth was to begin. This was to be the place where the soldiers would arrest Him, and soon afterward, He would be tried and crucified. The Bible tells us that as He wrestled in prayer, He literally perspired blood.

Jesus knew what was coming. Not only a horrific, humiliating death, but also separation from His Father. He would face the worse moments anyone could possibly face, alone (see Matt. 27:46). In the Garden of Gethsemane, He beseeched the Lord three times to "let this cup pass from Me."

Each time, though, He amended His prayer this way, "Yet not as I will, but as you will."

When we pray, are we willing to accept God's answer, no matter what it is? Are we totally submitted to God's will, regardless of what it may cost us?

Father, even in my most passionate pleadings, I pray that my spirit would come into agreement with Your will. . . .

My Thoughts

Pray with Confidence

"Let us then approach the throne of grace with confidence,
so that we may receive mercy and find grace to
help us in our time of need."
(Heb. 4:16)

Confidence is defined as "full belief in the trustworthiness or reliability of a person; the confiding of private matters; a confidential communication; and a confidential relationship."

In the *Wizard of Oz*, Dorothy, the Tin Man, the Lion, and the Scarecrow made a long and difficult journey in order to ask the wizard to grant their deepest, most desperate desires. But when they were finally granted an audience with him, it took everything they had not to flee in terror. They had no confidence coming before him because they had no idea what he would do. They had no prior relationship or friendship with him to help them predict his reaction.

When we stand before the throne of grace, however, there need be no fear and trembling. We can stand there with confidence because we know the nature of the King we pray to. We are there, in fact, by His invitation and desire.

"This is the confidence we have in approaching God: that if we ask anything according to his will, he hears us" (1 John 5:14).

Lord, thank You that I can approach Your throne of grace without fear, and with the confidence that You will welcome me and hear my prayer. . . .

My Thoughts

Pray Earnestly

"And without faith it is impossible to please God, because anyone who comes to him must believe that he exists and that he rewards those who earnestly seek him."
(Heb. 11:6)

The *Living Webster Encyclopedia of Words* defines *earnestly* as "with serious purpose, zealousness, or intensity."

Sometimes our prayers will be mere pleasure in God's company. Perhaps we're having coffee at the breakfast table, and a shaft of sunlight suddenly brightens the room; we hear birds singing, our husband humming as he gets ready for the day, the children going about their tasks, and we're suddenly thankful and at peace in a new day—so we share it with Him.

But other times, our prayers are more purposeful. We have an objective in praying, and we are earnestly seeking God's response.

When we pray with purpose, we envision the end result before it is accomplished. When we pray with zeal, we display an energy, excitement, and enthusiasm that shows God we believe He will answer. When we pray with intensity, we are focused on God and the objective of our prayer and nothing else.

As Richard Foster says, "Imagination opens the door to faith. If we can 'see' in our mind's eye a shattered marriage whole or a sick person well, it is only a short step to believing that it will be so."[2] And our faith pleases God, as does our earnestness.

Lord, I'm so glad that I can bring my deepest requests and longings to You, knowing that You welcome my vulnerability. . . .

My Thoughts

Pray in Faith—Part One

*"Then he touched their eyes and said, 'According to
your faith will it be done to you.'"*
(Matt. 9:29)

We don't know much about the two men in this
story, but we can deduce a few things from the short
account of their encounter with Jesus.

First, we know they were blind (Matt. 9:27); whether from
birth or from some sort of accident or disease, we can't tell.
Second, we know they cared for each other; they approached Jesus
together, and their request for mercy was a joint one. Third, we
know they had some idea who Jesus was; in verse 27, they call
Him "Son of David."

We also know they were bold. Jesus had been tugged at
from every side all day long by people wanting healing either
for themselves or for their loved ones (vv. 18-25). By the time
these two men got to Him, it appears that He had already
reached the house where He planned to retire for the night.
They followed Him, not only to the house, but also into the
house, persisting in their request. Finally Jesus turned to them,
and in their brief exchange we learn the most important thing
about them.

> Jesus said to them, "Do you believe that I am able
> to do this? They said to Him, "Yes, Lord." (v. 28,
> NASB)

The two men had faith. They believed that Jesus was able to restore their sight; the only question was whether He would choose to do so.

What few things might an observer glean from a brief glimpse into your prayer life? Would faith be among them?

Lord, grant me faith so that I can see. . . .

My Thoughts

Pray in Faith—Part Two

"If you have faith as small as a mustard seed . . .
nothing will be impossible for you."
(Matt. 17:20)

*Y*ears ago after my husband read this passage, I found him scrounging around in my spice cupboard. Several moments later he emerged with a bottle of tiny seeds—mustard seeds. Spilling them out, he stuck one seed onto a small portion of tape and disappeared without a word.

Later—and many times since—I noticed that small mustard seed taped to photos of our loved ones, the side of his desk, or a page in his Bible. Each time I see the mustard seed, I know that he is in fervent prayer for something. The mustard seed reminds him that his faith only needs to be that big—or small—to make a difference.

Mustard seeds may be tiny, but they produce enormous trees. Like a mustard seed, our faith can start out small, but grow into something great.

More importantly, though, it's not the size of our faith that makes the difference; it's who our faith is in.

Lord, sometimes my faith seems as minuscule as a mustard seed. Please help it germinate and grow! And in the meantime,

thank You that the size of my faith doesn't limit the greatness of Your actions. . . .

My Thoughts

Pray with Perseverance

"And will not God bring about justice for his chosen ones, who cry out to him day and night? Will he keep putting them off?"
(Luke 18:7)

*L*uke 18:1-8 recounts Jesus' parable of the persistent widow. She is in need of protection and appeals personally to the judge, who "neither feared God nor cared about men."

As the story unfolds, we find her continually returning to him with the plea, "Grant me justice against my adversary." The unjust judge tries to turn a deaf ear, but eventually he gives in to her, not out of compassion, but because she keeps bothering him!

Jesus then points out that, in contrast, we serve a just judge, one who does have compassion for us and will grant us justice if:

1. We are among His chosen (have accepted Him as our Lord and Savior), and

2. We cry out to Him day and night.

Sometimes it seems like justice—or help, or relief, or change—is slow in coming, even when our knees are sore from kneeling. We don't know why God sometimes delays His answers to us. Maybe it's because of the lessons we learn in the midst of struggle; perhaps because of the comfort and understanding we will one day be able to offer someone else; maybe it's simply because He wants us to rely on Him. Whatever the reason, there is something we do know: He values persistent prayer, ongoing prayer.

Try it yourself. Discover what benefits God has in store.

Help me, Lord, to persevere in my prayers, even when the answers don't appear to be coming. I trust You to hear me and to bring good from this time of waiting. . . .

My Thoughts

Pray While Fasting

"So we fasted and petitioned our God about this,
and he answered our prayer."
(Ezra 8:23)

Throughout the Bible, intense prayer is often accompanied by fasting. From the Old Testament, when Daniel fasted as he petitioned the Lord over the state of Jerusalem, to the New Testament, when Paul and Barnabas fasted over the sending out of elders, important events are often bathed in prayer and underlined by fasting.

Most of the time, the fasting occurs as a result of great mourning—often over the results of disobeying God. Repentance and the confession of sins followed. Other times, fasting is undertaken during times of deep trouble, or on days set aside to celebrate God's character. There are also examples of fasting so that God would reveal direction or grant a blessing. And just before entering into the temptation by the Devil, Jesus fasted for forty days.

Whatever prompts a fast, putting aside our earthly needs for a time allows us to concentrate on our heavenly purpose.

Thank You, Father, for providing spiritual nourishment. . . .

My Thoughts

Wrestle in Prayer

"[Epaphras] is always wrestling in prayer for you, that you may stand firm in all the will of God, mature and fully assured."
(Col. 4:12b)

What do you picture when you think of the word *wrestle?* Sweat, clenched jaws, straining muscles, gritty stamina?

What would it look like to wrestle in prayer?

In Genesis 32:22-32, Jacob wrestled all night with an angel, whom he later realizes is God. Jacob refused to let Him go until God blessed him. Finally, God not only gave Jacob His blessing, but also gave him a new name, Israel. It is clear in the passage that Jacob had earned God's admiration.

Have you ever wrestled with God in the middle of the night? Have you ever cried out to Him loudly in protest over circumstances in your life? Have you ever persisted in prayer, refusing to give up until God has given you what you ask? Have you ever wrestled with God on behalf of someone else?

We are not promised that when we wrestle with God, we will always win. But it is clear that God approves of strong feeling in our prayers. He likes fervency; He appreciates intensity. And He doesn't mind it when we stand up to Him.

God wants to engage with us, on the deepest level of our souls. He wants us to let Him into every nook, every cranny, every rage, every fear, every concern of our being. And when we do, like Jacob, we will be changed.

Lord, I want to hide nothing from You. Thank You for allowing me to bring You my deepest emotions and for engaging with me in the battles of my soul. . . .

My Thoughts

Make Prayer a Habit

*"Now when Daniel learned that the decree had been
published, he went home to his upstairs room where
the windows opened toward Jerusalem. Three times
a day he got down on his knees and prayed, giving
thanks to his God, just as he had done before."*
(Dan. 6:10)

King Darius reigned in Daniel's time. Daniel had
found such favor with him that the king was planning
to place Daniel in charge of the entire kingdom.
Others who wanted that position became jealous and tried to
find charges of wrongdoing or corruption that they could bring
against Daniel, but none were to be found.

Knowing that Daniel followed God, they set a trap for him.
Appealing to Darius' vanity, they convinced him to decree that,
for thirty days, no one could pray to anyone but him. Offenders
would be sent to the lions' den.

But the decree didn't change Daniel's routine at all. He continued to pray three times a day just as he always had. Eventually, he was thrown to the lions, and the rest of Daniel 6 tells
the story of how God saved him and restored his position in
Darius' kingdom.

Is your prayer life so strong that even the threat of death
wouldn't interfere with it?

Help me, Lord, to seek You continually. . . .

My Thoughts

Action Steps

Make an appointment with yourself to spend time each day in prayer. Look at your calendar each week in advance and make your prayer appointments. If you can schedule it for the same time every day, it will be easy to keep in a routine. Don't let any other appointment or interruption keep you from this most important appointment in your day.

Prepare a place on your "mountain" where you return every day for your time in prayer. You can even create a corner of a room with "your" chair, and a small stand where you can place your Bible and devotionals in preparation for prayer time. You might even want to light a scented candle, brew a cup of tea, and listen to soft Christian music to prepare your spirit and de-stress.

Keep a prayer journal to help you stay focused and as a record of what God is doing in your life.

Carry your journal notebook with you so that as people/needs/praises come to mind, you can write them down.

Enjoy this daily time with the Lord!

SECTION 4

Introduction
Where and When We Pray

an you imagine what the Garden of Eden must have looked like? When we think of the most incredible outdoor landscapes of today, they are but a clouded reflection of what God's original "church" looked like. This was the place that God created for man to learn from Him, ask questions, laugh with Him, and talk to Him—in other words, pray.

Unfortunately, Adam and Eve chose to disobey God, and the fearless, easy communication they had with Him changed. Separated from God by sin, people could no longer talk with Him face-to-face. Throughout the Old Testament, except in specific situations, people had to go through a priest to communicate with God, and the priest would come before an altar. Only certain men of God's own choosing were able to talk with Him in any other way.

During Moses' time, God did dwell again with His people, this time in a special tent rather than openly walking among them. But only the high priest was allowed to enter the inner part—the Holy of Holies—and even he could not look upon God's face. There the priest offered sacrifices for the people's sins so that God's relationship with them could continue. The people were instructed to pray twice each day—once in the morning and again in the evening. Now they had a place and time for prayer.

A thousand or more years passed before the New Testament ushered in a New Covenant. With Jesus offered as the sacrificial Lamb for all time, we no longer need to go through a high priest to talk to God; nor do we need to offer sacrifices to maintain our relationship with Him. It is no longer necessary to pray just twice a day at a particular location. Today, we can pray anywhere and at anytime! In fact, we now have the Holy Spirit who dwells within our souls, and we are, in effect, the walking temple of God. He resides in us!

The Bible, though, tells us of times and places in which others have chosen to pray. And it is these examples we are going to look at, because in them we can find new avenues of prayer to try and old ones in which to be encouraged.

When We Pray

When we pray there is an answer
When we pray the way seems clear
When we pray Jesus hears our cry
And takes away all our fear

Jesus' love can brighten up the darkest night
His forgiveness reaches way beyond the farthest, deepest sea
Jesus' blood can cleanse our wrongs and make them white

For He took away our sins at Calvary

When we pray there is an answer
When we pray the way seems clear
When we pray Jesus hears our cry
And takes away all our fear[1]

Paul and Timothy, at the Place of Prayer

"On the Sabbath we went outside the city gate to the river, where we expected to find a place of prayer."
(Acts 16:13)

Paul and Timothy were on a missionary journey that had taken them far from home and to many foreign cultures—some cultures, in fact, where Christianity was not welcome. We join them here in a Roman colony called Phillipi.

Phillipi was populated mostly by soldiers; they had been ordered to live there by Caesar Augustus in order to protect Roman interests in the area. There were apparently very few Jews living there, for there was no synagogue, which would have required only ten Jewish males.[2] Perhaps there was even an inscription on the city gates prohibiting any outside religions from worshiping inside the city walls. Instead, "a place of prayer," which may have been a place in the open air or a simple building, was located by the Gangites River about a mile and one-half west of town."[3] Paul and Timothy had been in Phillipi for several days, doing the work they had come to do, but now it is the Sabbath, a time for worship and prayer. Eventually, they will establish a church here, but for now, they seek out the closest thing they can find—this makeshift "place of prayer" on the river.

When you travel, do you tend to regard it as a break from the routine—even the routine of going to church? Or do you seek out other believers and make a special effort to find a "place of prayer?"

As believers, we have Christ in us wherever we go. A hotel room, a travel trailer, even a roadside park can serve as altars where we can spend time with Him. But Paul and Timothy chose to go where they might find others who believed as they did, and their time was more fruitful than they could have imagined (see Acts 16:13-15). On your next trip, why not try giving the Lord a chance to use or bless you in an unexpected way by attending a local church?

Lord, I know that a "place of prayer" exists within my own heart. Thank You for being with me wherever I go. . . .

My Thoughts

The Tribe of Reuben,
in the Heat of Battle

*"They were helped in fighting them . . . because they
cried out to him during the battle. He answered
their prayers, because they trusted in him."*
(1 Chron. 5:20)

*T*he tribe of Reuben was trying to establish its territory, and that meant fighting other people who also wanted land in that region. The sons of Reuben and all their offspring "were skillful in battle" (1 Chron. 5:18, NASB), but they knew where their real strength lay—in God. So they cried out to Him, and they won the war.

Most of us have never been involved in a war. At least, not a war with tanks and guns. Fighting probably isn't much a part of our way of life, other than a few skirmishes with husbands or kids, or maybe city hall.

It's easy for us to forget that we are involved in a spiritual war at all times. Our souls are territory Satan would like to claim. Ephesians 6 tells us that "our struggle is not against flesh and blood, but against the rulers, against the authorities, against the powers of this dark world and against the spiritual forces of evil in the heavenly realms" (v. 12). The Reubenites "bore shield and sword and shot with bow" (1 Chron. 5:18). Just as they did, we are supposed to put on our armor and take up our weapons. But also like the Reubenites, we need to "with all prayer and petition pray at all times" (Eph. 6:18, NASB).

Because prayer is our most powerful weapon.

Today, Lord, as I prepare for battle, I cry out to You, knowing that You will help me win. . . .

My Thoughts

Jehoshaphat, When He Was Helpless

"We have no power to face this vast army that is attacking us.
We do not know what to do, but our eyes are upon you."
(2 Chron. 20:12b)

As so often happened in Old Testament times, a "vast army" was out to get the nation of Israel.

As soon as Jehoshaphat heard that the army was coming, he knew his people were beaten. He didn't bother getting military advice; instead, he "resolved to inquire of the Lord, and he proclaimed a fast for all Judah" (2 Chron. 20:3). The people came from all over Judah to join in seeking help from the Lord, and verses 6 through 12 record the beautiful and desperate public prayer that Jehoshaphat led them in. He began with acknowledging God's might (v. 6); he went on to remind God of His past faithfulness (v. 7); and he beseeched the Lord to help His people (vv. 7-12). He ended with the words of a man at the end of his own abilities: "We do not know what to do, but our eyes are upon you."

And God came through. Verses 13-30 tell how God defeated the enemy, even leaving Judah better off than it was before; there was so much valuable plunder from the defeated army that it took the people of Judah three days to collect it all.

Have you ever come to the end of your resources and not known what else to do? That's the time to pray . . . and then stand back and see what He does.

Lord, I come to You empty handed, with no idea what to try next. Like Jehoshaphat, my eyes are upon You. I know You have a plan in store. . . .

My Thoughts

Jesus, at Mealtime

"Taking the five loaves and the two fish and looking up to heaven, he gave thanks and broke the loaves."
(Matt. 14:19b)

*I*f you know only one Bible story, this is probably it. Jesus had been preaching and healing all day out in a remote area, and the people who had followed Him there were surely getting hungry. The disciples suggested that He send them back to town where they could get some food. But Jesus performed His famous miracle, and the small amount of bread and fish they had with them became enough to feed more than five thousand—with leftovers! But before they ate, Jesus first "gave thanks."

Have you ever thought about where the practice of saying grace comes from? Maybe it's from this passage, and others like it.

It's easy to think of God as being concerned with how we're doing spiritually, but the Bible is full of examples of His concern for the state of our stomachs. He provided manna for the Israelites in the desert. On more than one occasion, Jesus fed the multitudes who followed Him. And we're admonished time and time again to feed the hungry.

Having enough food was probably a greater concern in Bible times than it is for most of us today. With refrigerators full of grapes becoming raisins and last week's chicken turning into a science experiment, it's easy to take our overstuffed bellies for granted. Yet even Jesus, who was capable of producing food where there was none, took the time to thank His Father before eating.

Mealtimes are good times to stop and reflect on all the practical ways God takes care of us.

Lord, thank You for the bread on my table, and thank You even more for the Bread of Life. . . .

My Thoughts

Elisha, Behind Closed Doors

*"He went in, shut the door on the two of
them and prayed to the Lord."*
(2 Kings 4:33)

*I*n 2 Kings 4 we're told a poignant story of friendship
and tragedy; it also opens a window onto a private
scene of passionate prayer.

Elisha was a prophet who traveled about proclaiming God's
Word. In Shunem, a place he visited regularly, he was befriended
by a wealthy but childless couple who actually added a room
onto their house for him to use when he was in their area.
Because of their kindness, God blessed them with a son.

Imagine the delight that longed-for child brought to this
couple! But one day, the little boy became ill, finally dying in
his mother's arms. She laid his body on Elisha's bed, mounted a
donkey, and rode fifteen miles to Mount Carmel to find "the
man of God."

This woman's dearness to Elisha is evident when he sees her
coming (vv. 25-26). He immediately sent his servant to try to
revive the child—but to no avail. When Elisha himself arrived,
there was nothing left to do but pray. But Elisha's prayer time
isn't just any prayer time. The account displays intensity, dis-
tress, persistence, and obedience.

When Elisha reached the house, there was the boy
lying dead on his couch. He went in, shut the door

on the two of them and prayed to the Lord. Then he got on the bed and lay upon the boy, mouth to mouth, eyes to eyes, hands to hands. As he stretched himself out upon him, the boy's body grew warm. Elisha turned away and walked back and forth in the room and then got on the bed and stretched out upon him once more. The boy sneezed seven times and opened his eyes (vv. 32-35).

This scene isn't intended as a model of how to revive the dead. It's just a picture. A picture of a man closing the door so that he could pray undistracted. A picture of a man doing seemingly odd things, apparently in response to what he was told in prayer. A picture of a man pacing and evidently persisting in prayer. A picture of a man obeying and becoming the instrument of a miracle.

Heavenly Father, help me to respond to desperate situations not with panic, but with focused, attentive prayer. And help me to act upon what You direct me to do. . . .

My Thoughts

_____

_____

_____

_____

Stephen, Facing Death

*"While they were stoning him, Stephen prayed,
'Lord Jesus, receive my spirit.'"*
(Acts 7:59)

Stephen was not one of the original twelve disciples, but as Christianity spread, he was one of the seven men appointed by the Twelve to help with the ministry (Acts 6:1-7). "A man full of grace and power" who "did great wonders and miraculous signs among the people," he quickly began to draw the attention and opposition of some powerful Jews (vv. 8-10). And they brought him before the Sanhedrin on trumped-up charges of blasphemy.

Given the opportunity to defend himself, he instead gave them a lengthy lecture on Jewish history and a scathing rebuke regarding their ironic and historic hindrance of God's work on their behalf (7:2-53). Instead of appeasing them, he made them furious by pointing out the truth. Wild with anger, "they all rushed at him, dragged him out of the city and began to stone him" (vv. 57-58).

But Stephen was faithful to the finish. Even as he was dying, he was doing the work he had been given; his last words were a prayer on behalf of the very men who were taking his life (v. 60)—an inspiring example. A calming example, though, are the words he spoke just prior to those: "Lord Jesus, receive my spirit" (v. 59).

To Stephen, death wasn't something to dread or fear; it was

just a transition, a short journey to a better place. Do you view death that way? Let Stephen's prayer help you face that time with confidence and even joy so that you can pray with him, "Lord, I'm on my way, and I can't wait!"

Lord, thank You that even in death You are with me, waiting to welcome me with outstretched arms. . . .

My Thoughts

Paul and Silas, with Their Backs Against the Wall

*"About midnight Paul and Silas were praying
and singing hymns to God."*
(Acts 16:25)

Acts 16:16-40 tells the story of a time when Paul and Silas were in prison. They had cast an evil spirit out of a girl who made money for her masters as a fortune-teller, and her owners had gotten mad. In retaliation, they got Paul and Silas beaten, stripped, and locked up in the most secure prison cell, their feet in stocks. There appeared to be no way out of this situation; there was even a jailer guarding them.

But Paul and Silas weren't wringing their hands. They weren't even commiserating with each other. Instead, they were holding a midnight sing-along and praying! Before long, an earthquake broke everyone's chains, the doors flew open, and the jailer became a Christian.

God doesn't always bail us out of difficult situations, though, even when we pray. More often, He chooses to use them in our lives to develop maturity (James 1:2-4). But that doesn't mean He leaves us to fend for ourselves. He is always with us, always working on our behalf, causing even negative situations to work out for our benefit (Rom. 8:28).

When your back is against the wall, when there seems to be no hope of a happy ending, do what Paul and Silas did:

Rejoice in the Lord always. . . . Do not be anxious about anything, but in everything, by prayer and petition, with thanksgiving, present your requests to God (Phil. 4:4-6).

If you will do that, you may not see the doors fly open or your chains fall off, but you will most certainly experience "the peace of God, which transcends all understanding" (v. 7).

Lord, when my back is against the wall—and even when it isn't—I want to turn to You. Grant me the peace that comes from knowing You will never leave me. . . .

My Thoughts

Action Steps

Wherever we are, whatever we are doing, we can pray and God will hear us. But perhaps this section has inspired you to pray in circumstances you hadn't thought of before, or in places or ways that you had not tried or had forgotten about.

Did any of the circumstances you read about remind you of your own? Maybe you have felt as if your back is to the wall, or that you are fighting a losing battle, or that you are helpless or without hope. Perhaps you are even facing death. Take some time to describe your circumstance here.

Did the stories give you ideas of how you might approach God in this matter? Write out your prayer here.

Have you ever considered seeking out a place of worship while traveling? Do you ever pray on your knees, or behind closed doors? Do you pray before meals? Write out your thoughts about these types of prayer.

Introduction
Intercessory Prayer

When the Israelites were wandering in the wilderness, delayed by their disobedience getting to the Promised Land, they were attacked by the Amalekites. Moses told Joshua to choose some men to fight, and he went up to the top of a hill overlooking the battle with the staff of God in his hands (Ex. 17:8-9).

There, an odd thing happened. "As long as Moses held up his hands, the Israelites were winning, but whenever he lowered his hands, the Amalekites were winning" (v. 11). The only problem was, Moses' arms got tired! So Aaron and Hur, who had gone up the hill with him, gave him a stone to sit on and held his hands up for him, "one on one side, one on the other" (v. 12). And the Israelites won the battle.

This story may not be about prayer, but the beautiful picture it paints gives us an image of what intercessory prayer is like. Intercessory prayer is simply praying on another's behalf; it means taking on the burden of another in our prayers. The ultimate prayer intercessor, of course, is the Holy Spirit; Romans 8:26 tells us that even when we can't find the words to pray, "the Spirit himself intercedes for us with groans that words cannot express." But we are also invited to intercede for others in prayer.

Joshua won a visible battle that day against the Amalekites. And we, too, can win battles in the spiritual realm when we hold others up in prayer. Let's look to the Scriptures for inspiration.

He Is Faithful

In a dark and lonely moment
A heart cries out in pain
The trials and the failures
Make it seem like all's in vain
When the world seems not to notice
When it looks like no one cares
A spark ignites a candle
For there's a God who hears our prayers

The light from that small candle
Allows our eyes to see
The miracles and wonders
Stretching to eternity
And when this life is over
When all is said and done
His works light up the heavens
Like brilliant diamonds in the sun

For He is faithful
God is faithful

God is faithful
He is standing close beside us
Waiting patiently to guide us
He is faithful
God is faithful
And His spirit is descending
With a love that is unending
He is faithful
Faithful, God is faithful

His light shines bright in the darkest night
And I know He holds my hand
Everywhere He's there and He shows His care
And I know He understands[1]

We Can Pray for Younger Believers

"We have not stopped praying for you and asking God to fill you with the knowledge of his will through all spiritual wisdom and understanding."
(Col. 1:9b)

These words are found near the beginning of a letter Paul wrote while in jail to a young but thriving church in Colosse. Paul had most likely never visited Colosse, nor even met the Colossian believers, but he knew of them through his friend Epaphras, who had traveled with Paul and had possibly even been imprisoned with him at one time. The reports of this church were glowing; however, Paul was concerned about the false teaching that was being spread in their area. One facet of that false teaching was the idea that "some special or deeper knowledge"[2] was needed for true spirituality.

And so, sitting in prison, he prayed on their behalf, addressing their needs in a specific way, asking that God give them knowledge and wisdom and understanding—exactly what they needed to counteract the false doctrine circulating among them.

In another letter, Paul asks us, too, to pray for other believers: "I urge, then, first of all, that requests, prayers, intercession and thanksgiving be made for everyone" (1 Tim. 2:1). We live in a time when unbiblical ideas abound, and young believers, especially, are vulnerable to confusion, just as the Colossians were. Let's make it a point to pray for them as Paul did.

Lord, please guard the hearts and minds of the young people in my church. Give them the wisdom they need in order to sort through the wide array of ideas that are set before them, and help them to choose the truth. . . .

My Thoughts

We Can Pray for Our Enemies

"Pray for those who mistreat you."
(Luke 6:28b)

This passage from Luke is full of instructions that stick in our craw: "Love your enemies, do good to those who hate you, bless those who curse you, pray for those who mistreat you."

Could there be anything harder? When people mistreat us, our first inclination is to retaliate; we feel pretty good if we're able to just bite our tongue and put the incident out of our mind. But *pray* for them? *"Implore God's blessing"* upon them? You've got to be kidding.

Proverbs 25:21-22 adds to that idea: "If your enemy is hungry, give him food to eat; if he is thirsty, give him water to drink. In doing this, you will heap burning coals on his head, and the Lord will reward you." *The Bible Knowledge Commentary* gives us some insight into the meaning of the passage.

> Sometimes a person's fire went out and he needed to borrow some live coals to restart his fire. Giving a person coals in a pan to carry home "on his head" was a neighborly, kind act; it made friends, not enemies. Also the kindness shown in giving someone food and water makes him ashamed of being an enemy, and brings God's blessing on the benefactor. Compassion, not revenge, should characterize

believers. . . . Alternately, light on this passage may come from an Egyptian expiation ritual, in which a person guilty of some wrongdoing would carry a pan of burning coals on his head as a sign of his repentance. Thus treating one's enemy kindly may cause him to repent.[3]

Praying for our enemies has the potential to change their hearts; but whether it does or not, it's still the right thing to do. God doesn't ask us to control the evil behavior of another and make it good; He requires us to do the right thing whether we have been wronged or not.

Lord, it's hard for me to ask this, but I do ask You to bless those who mistreat me. Help me to treat them right even when they treat me wrong. . . .

My Thoughts

We Can Pray for Our Friends

"I pray for . . . those you have given me."
(John 17:9)

*J*ohn 17 contains what is probably the best-known and best-loved prayer of intercession in the Bible. Jesus prayed it shortly before the end of His ministry and His life, and it is perhaps the most personal glimpse we're given into His heart.

The longest section of the prayer is on behalf of His best friends, the disciples (John 17: 6-19). This was one of the last opportunities He would have to pray for them, so His requests take on a special significance and poignancy. In these few verses, He asked God to give them the kind of unity with each other that He has with the Father (v. 11); joy, even in His absence (v. 13); protection from Satan (v. 15); and sanctification (vv. 17-19).

Certainly, the disciples will need all these things in order to carry on the ministry when Jesus is no longer physically present with them. But it is impossible to read this prayer and consider it "business only." The affection He feels for these men wells from every word, and it's plain that His requests arise not only from His concern for the ministry, but also from His personal interest in each man's well-being.

Each of us has special people in our lives—friends, teachers, family members, neighbors—whom God has gifted us with. What things might we ask God for on their behalf?

Heavenly Father, thank You for the people You've placed in my life. Please give to them the things Jesus prayed for His disciples to have. . . .

My Thoughts

_____

_____

_____

_____

_____

_____

_____

_____

_____

_____

_____

_____

_____

_____

We Can Pray for Those in Sin

"In accordance with your great love,
forgive the sin of these people."
(Num. 14:19)

his scene opens with Joshua and Caleb returning to the desert-wandering Israelites with a report of the Promised Land. They describe it as a land flowing with milk and honey, but also overflowing with enemies. The Israelites, despite the miracles they had witnessed one after another on their journey, despite God's promise to give their enemies into their hands, immediately burst into tears: "If only we had died in Egypt. Or in this desert! Why is the Lord bringing us to this land only to let us fall by the sword?" (Num. 14:2-3). They've complained about one thing after another ever since their rescue from slavery to the Egyptians, and now they're complaining about their new home. Wonderful as it is, they'd rather be dead or go back into slavery than than fight for it (v. 4).

And finally, God has had it. He vents to Moses, "How long will these people treat me with contempt? How long will they refuse to believe in me, in spite of all the miraculous signs? . . . I will strike them down with a plague and destroy them, but I will make you into a nation greater and stronger than they" (vv. 11-12).

Wow! Can you imagine it? Finally, Moses could be done with all of the whining and grumbling; he could be the leader of an even greater nation; he could live a life devoid of all the troubles of these unfaithful people! What's there to think about?

But Moses has learned from God's graciousness over the years, and he intercedes for them. First he appeals to logic, reminding God that other tribes are watching; if He kills the Israelites, they will say it was because He wasn't powerful enough to defeat them on the Israelites' behalf (vv. 13-16). Next, He reminds God of what He has said about Himself, that He is "slow to anger, abounding in love and forgiving sin and rebellion" (v. 18). "In accordance with your great love, forgive the sin of these people, just as you have pardoned them from the time they left Egypt until now" (v. 19).

Because of Moses' appeal, God tempers His judgment of the people. Perhaps, as a result of our prayers, He will temper His judgment of those we know who are in sin as well.

Lord, please show Your mercy to those around me who are locked in sin, and lead them back to You. . . .

My Thoughts

_____

_____

_____

_____

_____

We Can Pray for Another's Salvation

"I will go up to the Lord; perhaps I can
make atonement for your sin."
(Ex. 32:30)

When Moses returned to the camp after receiving the Ten Commandments, he found that the people had sinned against God by creating an idol in the form of a golden calf, and they were running around wild and worshiping it (Ex. 32:19-25). (Ironically, the first commandment from the tablets Moses carried stated that "You shall have no other gods before me" [20:3]).

Moses was understandably furious. He threw the tablets down and they broke into pieces; then he asked that anyone who was still for the Lord come and join him at the entrance to the camp. Only the Levites came. All the rest, about three thousand, were killed. The next day, Moses reminded the people who were left that they, too, had committed a great sin, but told them that he would go and try to make atonement for them before the Lord (v. 30).

Atonement has often been defined by the word itself: *at-one-ment.* It means performing some action that will make up for a wrong done and restore the relationship between two people—or, in this case, between a group of people and their God.

So strong was Moses' desire for the children of Israel to be forgiven that he offered his own life in exchange for God's mercy upon them: "But now, please forgive their sin—but if not, then blot me out of the book you have written"(v. 32). You see, under the law that Moses had been given, a blood sacrifice was required in atonement for sins.

In the New Testament, Jesus Christ fulfilled once and for all the requirement of atonement on our behalf. We cannot accept that gift on behalf of other people, but we can certainly pray that they will come to accept it for themselves.

Lord, move me with compassion for the lost as Moses was moved. Please make Yourself known to them and draw them to Yourself. . . .

My Thoughts

We Can Pray out of Compassion

"Isaac prayed to the Lord on behalf of his wife,
because she was barren."
(Gen. 25:21)

*I*saac was the son of Abraham and Sarah, given to them in their old age to fulfill God's promise to Abraham regarding his lineage. Isaac was forty years old before he married, and even though he became engaged to Rebekah sight unseen, it became a relationship of love (Gen. 24:67). So when Rebekah was unable to conceive, Isaac ached for her.

Of course, he was probably hurting for himself, as well. No doubt he wanted a family too; but then, we have to remember, he grew up in the home of Abraham and Sarah. He had surely been told of the unusual circumstances of his own birth, and he had to have known about the promise God had made to his father—that his offspring would outnumber the stars in the sky. So Isaac was probably fairly confident that God would come through eventually. And we see where his real concern lay in the wording of the verse: he prayed "on behalf of his wife." Not on his own behalf, not on behalf of God's promise to his father, but on behalf of Rebekah.

Anyone who has been loved as Isaac loved Rebekah—or who longs to be loved in that way—knows that the real blessing of this prayer was not in its answer, but in its existence. God was already planning to give Rebekah children, as Isaac knew. In this case, Isaac was praying from his heart, not his head.

We cannot control the answer God chooses to our prayers, although we see many examples in Scripture of prayer changing God's mind. But caring for someone enough to pray on his or her behalf is balm itself.

Lord, let my heart be full of compassion so that I can pray on others' behalf. . . .

My Thoughts

We Can Pray for God to Open Someone's Eyes

"And Elisha prayed, 'O Lord, open his eyes so he may see.'"
(2 Kings 6:17)

A tribe called the Arameans were at war with Israel, but they weren't having much success. Elisha, with ability from God, kept telling the king of Israel where the Arameans were camped. This infuriated the king of Aram, and he sent troops to surround the city where Elisha was staying, hoping to capture the prophet and put a stop to his interference.

The next morning, when Elisha woke up, the city was surrounded by the enemy. His servant panicked, but Elisha stayed calm. "Don't be afraid," he told his servant. "Those who are with us are more than those who are with them" (2 Kings 6:16). And then Elisha prayed for his servant's eyes to be opened.

> Then the Lord opened the servant's eyes, and he looked and saw the hills full of horses and chariots of fire all around Elisha (v. 17).

These were, of course, angels, protecting the "man of God," as Elisha was known—and thus, protecting Israel.

Like Elisha's servant, we often have trouble seeing things from God's perspective. We see the natural world around us and forget that there is anything more.

When our loved ones and friends have lost sight of the truth, we need to pray, "O Lord, open their eyes so they will see!"

Lord, open our eyes so we may see. . . .

My Thoughts

We Can Pray for Others' Protection

*"[Samuel] cried out to the Lord on Israel's behalf,
and the Lord answered him."
(1 Sam. 7:9)*

*I*n 1 Samuel 7, the Israelites, once again in need of repentance, have gathered at Mizpah. Having put away their foreign gods, they are fasting and confessing their sins, and Samuel offers to intercede with the Lord for them. Things seem to be going well, until the Philistines find out what they are doing and decide to attack them.

Samuel, having heard about their plans, now goes before the Lord on a different matter—requesting protection for the Israelites. He made a burnt offering, then "cried out to the Lord on Israel's behalf, and the Lord answered him" (v. 9). As the Philistines "drew near to engage Israel in battle . . . the Lord thundered with loud thunder against the Philistines and threw them into such a panic that they were routed before the Israelites" (v. 10).

Our enemy isn't always as easy to identify. Satan is on the attack against each of us, wanting to destroy our lives and to deceive us concerning the power available to us through our relationship with Jesus Christ—but he does it in such subtle ways that we don't see him coming. Like Samuel, we need to intercede for other believers so that our enemy will be defeated.

Lord, I pray Your hand of protection today on my closest family and friends. . . .

My Thoughts

We Can Pray to Save a Nation

*"Let your ear be attentive and your eyes open to hear the
prayer your servant is praying before you day and night for
your servants, the people of Israel. I confess the sins
we Israelites, including myself and my father's
house, have committed against you."*
(Neh. 1:6)

Approximately 438 years have passed since Solomon
built the great temple in Jerusalem, and now it has
come to Nehemiah's attention that the walls and
gates of the city are in disrepair. More importantly, though, he
realizes that in those 400 years, the nation Israel has crumbled
time and time again because of its disobedience to God.

First and Second Kings give a chronology and history of the
kings who reigned between around 1010 B.C. and 586 B.C. It is
interesting to note that each time a king was disobedient, God
would destroy almost the entire nation. However, at the end of
many accounts of exile and destruction, God left a remnant of
His people to provide the lineage for Christ.

So now, when Nehemiah becomes aware of the sad state of
Israel and the gates of her city, he intercedes in prayer, on behalf
of both the scattered remnant and the city of Jerusalem. He asks
God to forgive the people's sins, and in effect, give them another
chance at being recognized as a nation—a nation that worships
God.

God honored Nehemiah's prayer of intercession. He did so because Nehemiah was a man of action. God knew that he would give more than just lip service to uniting a nation; he would fight for it.

It is symbolic that Nehemiah's intercession accomplished the rebuilding of a literal wall (in only fifty-two days!). However, his faithful action led to a spiritual rebuilding of the nation of Israel as well. Perhaps if we will pray on behalf of our sinful nation, God will listen and help us turn back to Him as well.

Lord, please forgive the sins of our nation and help us to rebuild our spiritual walls. . . .

My Thoughts

Action Steps

If you know of others who routinely intercede for you in prayer, list their names here and pray for them today. Thank the Lord for their faithfulness in praying for you, and then intercede on their behalf to the Lord.

_____

_____

_____

_____

_____

List the names of others for whom you can intercede in prayer this week.

- Family _____
- Friends _____
- Coworkers _____
- Neighbors _____
- Church Leaders/Missionaries _____
- Government Officials _____
- Teachers and School Administrators _____

As you pray for these individuals, be sure to include:

- Thanksgiving and praise to God for these people
- Requests for their spiritual condition/growth
- Prayer for their needs to be met

- Help in your attitudes and acceptance of those you are praying for
- Thanksgiving and praise to God for what He will do

Section 6

Introduction
Things That Hinder Prayer

*H*ave there been times when you've prayed and prayed over a matter, only to feel that your words must be disappearing into a void somewhere? Sometimes it seems as though our prayers come back to us marked "Return to Sender"—unheard, unanswered.

It's hard not to feel disappointed at those times, or even to wonder whether God really does listen or care. We know that "[His] thoughts are not [our] thoughts, neither are [our] ways [His] ways" (Isa. 55:8)—but still . . . sometimes our request just seems so reasonable, so necessary and good. How could He possibly have a better idea?

Sometimes our requests involve other people, to whom God has given free will; sometimes what we can learn while waiting is more valuable than the answer itself. Sometimes what we're asking for is a good thing at the wrong time. And sometimes, He really does have a better idea. Years ago, my husband lost his job. We prayed and prayed that God would open up a job in the same city so we wouldn't have to move, change churches, and leave our friends. Well, thank God for unanswered prayer! Just days before our lease was up, he was offered a job in a different city. Reluctant as we were to go, God had blessings in store for us there that we could not have predicted. With hindsight, we can see that His way truly was better.

But sometimes, our prayers are not answered because of things within our control. Not always, but sometimes. If you find that your prayers seem to be bouncing off the ceiling, take a look at your heart. You may find something there that is undermining the effectiveness of your prayers. In this section, we'll take a look at what some of those things might be.

The Father Cares for You

The Father cares for you more than words can ever say
And He's here to meet with you today
For He knows your heartache and your need
He wants to wipe your tears away

The Father cares for you. His love is here to stay
He will never leave or turn away
For what He promised He will do for you
He can turn your night to day

Jesus walked that road to Calvary
To die for you and me!
Oh how He cares for you and He will be there through
Your joys and sorrows too
Oh how He loves you. Oh how Jesus cares for you![1]

Prayer Blocker 1: Disobedience

*"You rebelled against the Lord's command. . . . You came
back and wept before the Lord, but he paid no attention
to your weeping and turned a deaf ear to you."*
(Deut. 1:43, 45)

The Israelites had been wandering around in the
desert for forty years, kept out of the Promised Land
because of their disobedience. Finally, they had reached
the outskirts of this wonderful place, but once again, they were
in trouble. In Deuteronomy 1, Moses reviewed with the people
why this was so.

They were supposed to enter the Promised Land and fight
whatever tribes lived there, but they were intimidated to do that.
So Moses tried to ease their fears with a message from God: "Do
not be terrified; do not be afraid of them. The Lord your God,
who is going before you, will fight for you, as he did for you in
Egypt, before your very eyes, and in the desert. There you saw
how the Lord your God carried you, as a father carries his son, all
the way you went until you reached this place" (vv. 29-31).

But the Israelites grumbled in their tents like crabby children. "The Lord hates us; so he brought us out of Egypt to deliv-
er us into the hands of the Amorites to destroy us" (v. 27). And
they refused to go.

Because of their disobedience, the Lord decided that they
would never get to go into the Promised Land; only Joshua and

the children too young to know good from bad would be allowed in. Even Moses was stuck outside with them (vv. 37-39).

Of course, then the Israelites changed their minds. They packed up their weapons and headed into the hill country—and lost the battle. God had said, "Do not go up and fight, because I will not be with you. You will be defeated by your enemies" (v. 42). In fact, the enemy "chased [them] like a swarm of bees and beat [them] down from Seir all the way to Hormah" (v. 44). Then they came running back and wept before the Lord, but it was too late. The Lord "paid no attention to [their] weeping and turned a deaf ear to [them]" (v. 45).

God is full of grace, but He also expects us to obey. Have you said no to something you know the Lord wants you to do? Or have you gone running off to fight a battle or start a project without the Lord's okay? If so, you can hardly expect His blessing on it! Back up a little. Check in with the master plan. See which way He'd like you to turn next.

Father, with all my heart I want to be obedient—to the words You've recorded in the Bible, and to the words You write on my heart. Help me to hear You and to obey. . . .

My Thoughts

Prayer Blocker 2: Doubt

*"If any of you lacks wisdom, he should ask God . . .
and it will be given to him. But when he asks,
he must believe and not doubt."*
(James 1:5-6)

How many times have we come to a crossroads and wondered which way to turn—this job or that job, this man or that one, stay or move? How often have we been faced with a circumstance we didn't know how to handle regarding a child or a spouse or a coworker?

If you've been there, you know what it's like to want wisdom. *"What should I do?"* is the cry of our hearts at those times.

Our greatest store of wisdom actually comes from a pretty unmystical source. It's found in black and white on the pages of our Bibles, and the better acquainted we are with it, the less often we will feel desperate for answers—we'll already know the principles; it will be just a matter of applying them to our current situation. And when advice or ideas come to us, we can weigh them against what we know to be true in Scripture.

So often, we cry out for wisdom, beg for it, think maybe we've received it . . . then doubt it! Was God really speaking through that friend? The thoughts that came to me as I was praying—were those really from God? The passage of Scripture that leapt out at me—was that really related to my situation?

If you ask for wisdom, believe you're going to receive it—

and look for it. Otherwise, you'll be "like a wave of the sea, blown and tossed by the wind" (v. 6). And you'll feel as if your prayer was never answered.

Lord, I'm so grateful that I don't have to face decisions alone. Help me to know Your voice and respond to it. . . .

My Thoughts

Prayer Blocker 3: Hypocrisy

*"And when you pray, do not be like the hypocrites, for
they love to pray standing in the synagogues and on
the street corners to be seen by men. I tell you the
truth, they have received their reward in full."*
(Matt. 6:5)

We get our word *hypocrite* from the Greek theater,
where actors were called "hypocrites" because they
pretended to be someone they were not.

In Scripture, one of the most dramatic examples of hypocrisy
involved the scribes and the Pharisees. They were the Jewish
religious leaders who had all of the outward trappings of piety.
However, they were so corrupt on the inside that Jesus rebuked
them by saying, "Woe to you, teachers of the law and Pharisees,
you hypocrites! You shut the kingdom of heaven in men's faces.
You yourselves do not enter, nor will you let those enter who are
trying to" (Matt. 23:13-14).

Hypocrites share several characteristics: they know the truth,
but don't obey it; their motives are self-serving; they claim to be
someone they aren't; they try to impress others; they disguise
their sinful motives and present them as religious. In other
words, a hypocrite is a liar, and God detests liars.

Man sees the outside, but God knows the inside. Who is it
that we need to impress, people or God? It's time to take off the
mask and quit pretending. God honors a sincere heart.

Lord, I come to You privately and sincerely, as the person I really am. Please hear my prayer. . . .

My Thoughts

Prayer Blocker 4: Pride

*"For everyone who exalts himself will be humbled,
and he who humbles himself will be exalted."
(Luke 18:14)*

This verse closes one of Jesus' parables. In it, Jesus made His point by telling the story of two men: a Pharisee (religious leader) and a tax collector (typically, someone who cheated people out of more money than they owed and kept the difference). In the story, the Pharisee prayed out in public, using his prayer as a means of bragging on himself, thanking God that he wasn't a sinner like other people and making sure to mention that he fasted twice a week and tithed (Luke 18:10-12).

The tax collector, though, stood at a distance. "He would not even look up to heaven, but beat his breast and said, 'God, have mercy on me, a sinner'" (v. 13).

The Pharisee and the tax collector were both sinners; in that regard, they were just alike. The difference between them lay in their awareness of their sin. Jesus couldn't care less about the Pharisee's tithing and fasting. What He appreciated was the tax collector's humility.

"I tell you that this man [the tax collector], rather than the other, went home justified before God" (v. 14).

Lord, in the privacy of my prayer closet, I humble myself, a sinner, before You. . . .

My Thoughts

Prayer Blocker 5: Selfishness

*"When you ask, you do not receive, because you
ask with wrong motives, that you may spend
what you get on your pleasures."*
(James 4:3)

*W*ait a minute—is this saying God doesn't want us
to ask for anything we might enjoy?

It helps to know what is meant by the words
spend and *pleasures*. The word *spend* could be translated *squander*.
Pleasure is translated from the Greek word *hedonais*—we would
say *hedonistic*.[2] So what this verse is telling us is that we are not
to fritter away the gifts God gives us on pursuits that serve no
purpose beyond self-indulgence. If that is our intent, we are not
likely to see answers to our prayers.

The trouble with selfishness is that its focus is limited—to
ourselves. It takes over room in our hearts that is meant to be
occupied with others—their needs, their desires, their hopes,
their dreams. Phillipians 2:4 puts it beautifully:

> Each of you should look not only to your own inter-
> ests, but also to the interests of others.

*Lord, take my selfish desires and replace them with desire for
You. Help me to use the gifts You've blessed me with for the
benefit of others. . . .*

My Thoughts

Prayer Blocker 6: Spiritual Warfare

"Since the first day that you set your mind to gain understanding and to humble yourself before your God, your words were heard, and I have come in response to them. But the prince of the Persian kingdom resisted me twenty-one days. Then Michael, one of the chief princes, came to help me."
(Dan. 10:12-13)

aniel had been visited by the angel Gabriel, who had given him a message concerning Israel's future. But Daniel was having trouble understanding the message, so he "mourned for three weeks. [He] ate no choice food; no meat or wine touched [his] lips; and [he] used no lotions at all until the three weeks were over" (Dan. 10:2-3). At the end of that time, another angel came to interpret the message for him.

Why did Daniel have to wait three weeks? Because the angel who had been sent to explain things to him was delayed by a spiritual battle (vv. 11-13). The passage reveals that there is a parallel, spiritual universe around us where warfare for our souls and for the kingdom of God is in full progress.

What's interesting to note in this story is that nothing had hindered Daniel's prayer from being heard by God; Daniel had worked hard to make sure that he was right with God as he prayed. The hang-up was in the answer getting to Daniel.

Could spiritual battle sometimes be the reason the answers to our prayers are delayed? What can we do to combat the spiritual forces that work against us?

Let's look at the way Jesus talked to the Devil when He was tempted in the desert. In the Matthew 4 account, Jesus didn't rationalize, argue, or do physical battle with His adversary; He quoted Scripture. He began each rebuke with, "It is written." Finally, Jesus commanded, "Away from Me, Satan!"

Yes, there is a parallel spiritual universe surrounding us, and yes, answers to our prayers may be affected by it, but we can take comfort knowing that God always hears our prayers and that we are surrounded by legions of angels who are watching over us.

Lord, thank You for the angels who keep watch over us! Help me to be aware of the battle raging around me. . . .

My Thoughts

Prayer Blocker 7: Concern for Appearances

*"And when you pray, do not be like the hypocrites,
for they love to pray standing in the synagogues and
on the street corners to be seen by men. I tell you
the truth, they have received their reward in full."*
(Matt. 6:5)

We've all seen them and probably know some: the Large and in Charge! These are the people who want to impress us by who they know, what they know, and when they knew it. They maintain their perceived power through intimidation and visibility. They attend the right events and always appear in the photographs with the right people. There are people like this throughout society; the sad thing is, there are also people like this in the church.

The message of this verse is not that public praying is wrong. In fact, we are encouraged that "where two or three come together in my name, there am I with them" (Matt. 18:20). Instead, the message has to do with motive. Praying in public for the sake of looking spiritual is not really praying, and it accomplishes just what you would expect fake prayer to accomplish—nothing.

Jesus encourages us to spend time alone in prayer: "But when you pray, go into your room, close the door and pray to your Father, who is unseen. Then your Father, who sees what is done in secret, will reward you" (6:6). But the real issue is not a matter of place, but of the heart.

≈∽

Father, when I pray, whether privately or in public, please help me to talk to no one else but You. . . .

My Thoughts

Prayer Blocker 8: Wickedness

*"The Lord is far from the wicked but he
hears the prayer of the righteous."*
(Prov. 15:29)

What exactly qualifies as wickedness? Throughout the Old Testament, especially in Proverbs, the word *wickedness* is used in reference to the way people treat each other. A wicked person may be dishonest, violent, oppressive, engaging in extortion, fraudulent . . . the list goes on and on.

In 2 Chronicles 7:14-15, God tells Solomon some of the conditions under which He will answer His people's prayers. One of them is to "turn from their wicked ways"—in other words, repent. Not just say they're sorry, but change. Turn around and head in the other direction.

Is there anything wicked in the way you are dealing with other people? If so, change your ways. Until you do, you will feel as though God is far away.

Father, I confess that my dealings with other people are not always what they should be. I commit before You today that I will change. . . .

My Thoughts

Action Steps

Perhaps this long list of "don'ts" has you feeling as if you may as well quit before you begin! But don't forget the Israelites—a more sinful, stubborn group of people there never was. Yet God still loved them and gave them chance after chance to come before Him. As He Himself told Moses: "[I am] the Lord, the Lord, the compassionate and gracious God, slow to anger, abounding in love and faithfulness, maintaining love to thousands, and forgiving wickedness, rebellion and sin" (Ex. 34:6-7).

Don't we owe it to such a gracious God to make our best efforts to please Him? Instead of tossing your prayers His way as you hurry about your business, slow down. Take steps today to prepare yourself before going to God in prayer.

1. Confess and repent of all sin, and ask for God's forgiveness.

2. Examine your heart.

   • List any areas of continuing struggle or disobedience.

   • Examine your motives for praying.

   • Check your mind for doubt.

3. Spend some time in God's Word, showing Him that you are serious about following Him.

SECTION 7

Introduction
How to Hear God

*G*od is everywhere. He created us so that He could fellowship and communicate with us. He longs to speak to us and have us hear Him. So why do we sometimes feel that He's just not there?

The truth is, God speaks to us through almost everything we experience each day: nature, other people, circumstances, our thoughts, our "gut" feelings, our conscience. But when we get so wrapped up in our routine and the noise and confusion around us, His voice is often drowned out. He's speaking, all right; we just can't hear Him.

In Proverbs 8:17, God tells us that "those who diligently seek me will find me" (NASB). In this section, we will discover some ways to diligently seek God . . . and as we put them into practice, we will surely find Him.

Take Time to Pray

Take time to pray
Take time to humbly seek Him and obey
Take time to give your burdens all away

Take time to pray
Take time to learn God's perfect holy way
Take time to meet with the Savior every day
Take time to tell Him all your needs
Take time to listen as He leads
And He will give you strength to carry on

Take time to pray
Take time to learn God's perfect holy way
Take time to meet with the Savior every day[1]

Seek God by Getting to Know His Voice

"My sheep listen to my voice; I know
them, and they follow me."
(John 10:27)

I once attended a mother/daughter picnic with my daughter's Brownie troop. More than two hundred mothers and daughters attended; can you imagine how many times the frantic cry, "Mom," was heard? Yet in all the chaos, it was only when my daughter yelled out "Mom" that I responded. Among all the other voices, I recognized hers because I know it so well.

If we want to hear God speak to us, we have to get to know Him. The more time we spend in His presence, the more we read His Word, the more easily we will recognize His voice when He is trying to get our attention.

God's followers are described as sheep throughout the Bible. Not a very flattering analogy, in some regards! Generally speaking, sheep are helpless and dependent, apt to go astray, and they need to be guided to pastures and water. But if a sheep knows its shepherd's voice, it's in good shape. It's the sheep that thinks it can go it alone who gets itself in trouble!

We have a Shepherd who knows each one of us by name and by characteristics. He knows what is likely to distract us, and if we wander off, He goes after us to bring us back (see Luke 15:4-6).

All our lives, He is calling our name, guiding us with His staff, leading us to nourishment and safety. But sometimes we don't notice.

Maybe if we act more like the sheep we really are, we will be better able to hear the Shepherd's voice!

Lord, when I go astray, help me to hear Your voice. . . .

My Thoughts

Seek God by Doing Right

*"While you were doing all these things, declares the Lord,
I spoke to you again and again, but you did not listen;
I called you, but you did not answer."
(Jer. 7:13)*

*I*n the verses that precede this one, we discover that
the Israelites' disobedient actions had kept them from
hearing God: they stole, murdered, committed adultery
and perjury, and burned incense to other gods. Then they had
the audacity to come into God's holy temple. God accused them
of making His house into a den of robbers (the same term Jesus
used when He ransacked the temple in Matthew 21:13). They
had made a mockery of God's justice and grace.

Paul warned us about sinning against God when we know
better: "Shall we go on sinning so that grace may increase? By
no means!" (Rom. 6:1-2). Sin has a very distracting quality; not
only does it cheapen God's love for us, but it also makes it very
hard to hear His voice. Maybe because we really don't want to
hear God's voice when we are up to something we shouldn't be.

Jeremiah 7:3-7 tells us what we need to do if we truly want
to dwell in God's presence.

> Reform your ways and your actions, and I will let you
> live in this place. . . . If you really change your ways
> and your actions, and deal with each other justly, if
> you do not oppress the alien, the fatherless or the

widow and do not shed innocent blood in this place, and if you do not follow other gods to your own harm, then I will let you live in this place . . . for ever and ever.

Lord, keep me from sin so that I might stay near You. . . .

My Thoughts

Seek God in Worship

*"While they were worshiping the Lord and fasting,
the Holy Spirit said . . ."*
(Acts 13:2)

The New Testament word for worship in this verse means *to bow down to* or to show reverence to God. Although worship is a matter of our hearts, it is also an outward, public expression of the church's corporate relationship with God. One source reveals that the English word *worship* actually stemmed from the Old English term *worthship*, denoting that God is worthy of our praise.

Amazing things take place when we acknowledge God's power as our Creator and His love as our Savior. It is often during public worship that we hear God speak.

One of our TimeOut staff members is a fairly new Christian. Not having been raised in a Christian home, the public worship that took place at her fiancé's church was very foreign to her. At the end of one particular service, her fiancé was praying diligently that God would somehow give her a sign from the Holy Spirit that she could trust in the Lord as her personal Savior. As he was praying for her during the closing hymn, she felt as if the wind had been knocked right out of her and had to sit down in the pew to catch her breath! She knew, through this worship experience, that God was moving and preparing her for service to Him.

Could this experience have taken place at home in the

privacy of her prayer closet? Certainly. But God honors corporate worship and loves to work in our midst when we publicly give Him thanksgiving and praise for who He is.

Although the Jewish tradition was to keep the Sabbath (Saturday) holy, with the resurrection of Christ having taken place on Sunday, Christians began calling this the "Lord's Day" and meeting on this day to celebrate His resurrection. Jesus said, "For where two or three come together in my name, there am I with them" (Matt. 18:20). He blesses and speaks to us during worship.

Lord, I praise You for being in our midst during worship. . . .

My Thoughts

Seek God by Being Open to His Spirit

$\approx)\approx$

"Do not put out the Spirit's fire."
(1 Thess. 5:19)

Many times in the Bible, the Spirit is symbolized by fire. God spoke to Moses from a burning bush; He appeared as a pillar of fire to the children of Israel; on Mount Carmel, the Spirit descended as fire, consuming the sacrifices; when the Comforter came to the disciples, tongues of fire appeared on their heads.

Given the appropriate environment, a fire gives warmth, provides light, and can be passed on to give someone else warmth and light. Someone once observed that "a candle loses nothing of its light by lighting another candle."

Much of the fun of camping involves sitting around the campfire at night. Our family has often enjoyed toasting marshmallows and hot dogs over the open flame. However, when it's "lights out," we take several buckets of water and sand and douse the fire until it is completely extinguished.

Often, even though we want to hear from God, we douse the Spirit's flame within our hearts. We "put out" His voice through negative attitudes, worry, doubt, complaints, selfishness—in other words, sin! We quench His words rising up within us before they can ignite.

The Spirit's fire is intended as a gift that lives within us to provide us with warmth and light. It allows us to hear God.

Then, as we are warmed and guided by God's Spirit, it is our privilege to be able to pass His flame along.

≈)⊂≈

Lord, burn bright within me so that I may hear Your voice. . . .

My Thoughts

Seek God by Meditating

*"But his delight is in the law of the Lord, and on
his law he meditates day and night."*
(Ps. 1:2)

editating is a deliberate action. It means to think on something, to plan or intend or contemplate doing something. Meditating takes time. More than a daydream, it is a brainstorm, an analysis, a reflection. And it is often a medium through which God speaks to us. "Meditation has as its objective to bring you into a deep inner communion with the Father where you look at Him and He looks at you."[2]

In our busy lives, we seldom have time to think about much beyond where we need to be next. We snatch part of a radio sermon in the car, maybe speed-read a devotional book with our morning coffee, pray as we blow-dry our hair—and there is nothing wrong with any of that. But something different happens when we quiet ourselves and think, pondering a passage of Scripture or some troubling situation in our lives. When we invite God to sit quietly with us, He quite often speaks in our thoughts. We may come away with practical help, such as how to interact more effectively with our spouse, or we may come away with an inner glow, in wonder at having been in God's presence. As Frederick W. Faber puts it:

Only to sit and think of God,

Oh what a joy it is!

To think the thought, to breathe the Name

Earth has no higher bliss.[3]

Father, help me to slow down my life and take time to meditate on Your Word. . . .

My Thoughts

Seek God in Our Disabilities

*"But those who suffer he delivers in their suffering;
he speaks to them in their affliction."*
(Job 36:15)

*I*t has been conjectured that Moses was a stutterer because he admitted to being slow of speech. Jacob ended up walking with a limp after wrestling with the angel. Paul had his thorn in the flesh.

We all probably suffer from some kind of disability, whether physical or emotional. However, sometimes it is through that very disability that God speaks to us.

Joni Eareckson Tada (JAF Ministries) was paralyzed in a diving accident when she was seventeen years old. At a TimeOut for Women! conference, she spoke with fervor on the subject of suffering: "He will permit what He hates: He despises divorce, He hates cancer, He hates diabetes and spinal cord injury. But He will permit it. He will allow it to accomplish something in us which He treasures far more and which ultimately one day we will rejoice for as well. Suffering causes us to lean hard on Him when otherwise we would not."

It is ironic how a disability can take our focus off of ourselves and place it on God. It puts us in a dependent position where we have no other alternative but to lean on Him for answers, support, and peace. Our greatest liability becomes our most valuable asset because in it, we hear the voice of God.

Lord, help me to hear You through my disabilities. . . .

My Thoughts

Seek God Through His Word

> *"How sweet are your promises to my taste,*
> *sweeter than honey to my mouth."*
> *(Ps. 119:103)*

Take a few moments to read Psalm 119. Yes, it's the longest psalm, but time after time its contents refer to the secret of hearing God—through His own words! How do we keep from sinning? "I have hidden your word in my heart that I might not sin against you" (v. 11). "I meditate on your precepts and consider your ways. I delight in your decrees; I will not neglect your word" (vv. 15, 16).

Have you ever been so overloaded with sorrow that you felt exhausted? "My soul is weary with sorrow; strengthen me according to your word" (v. 28). Have you ever felt that you were in bondage to sin or affliction? "I will walk about in freedom, for I have sought out your precepts" (v. 45). Do you long to be comforted? "I remember your ancient laws, O Lord, and I find comfort in them" (v. 52).

Do you want to keep from going astray? "Before I was afflicted I went astray, but now I obey your word" (v. 67). Have you ever lost hope? "For I have put my hope in your word" (v. 74). Have you ever lost your way and wondered where, when, and how to take the next step? "Your word is a lamp to my feet and a light for my path" (v. 105). Have you ever longed to be protected? "You are my refuge and my shield; I have put my hope in your word" (v. 114).

Reading, meditating upon, and knowing God's Word allows us to hear Him during the times we need Him. When my father was passing away from cancer I remember sitting in the hospital room watching his life ebb away. As I looked upon this sweetest of men, it broke my heart to know his suffering, and the ultimate loss Mom and I would suffer. But God's Word through Scripture comforted me: "Blessed are those who mourn, for they will be comforted" (Matt. 5:4). And we truly have been . . .

Lord, help me to hear Your voice in a new way today through Your Word. . . .

My Thoughts

Seek God Through Jesus

⌒⌒

"In these last days he has spoken to us by his Son."
(Heb. 1:2)

A lthough God never changes, His revelations change us. Yet the way He speaks is different now than it was in the beginning.

In the Garden of Eden, God walked and talked freely with Adam and Eve until their actions invited sin into the world. This distanced them from God. In time, however, God spoke directly to many men, including Noah, Moses, and Joshua. He also chose certain godly men to speak on His behalf, men like the prophets Elisha and Elijah, Jeremiah, Samuel, and many others. Even angels at times appeared to people, announcing God's news or guiding and directing.

But when Jesus Christ came, man was able to see and hear God incarnate—His Spirit living in human form. From Jesus came words spoken straight from the heart of the Father. These words, having been recorded for us, give us a direct way to hear God's voice.

One interesting way to hear God is to read just Jesus' words—often printed in red—in the New Testament. Even if this were the only portion of the Bible available to us, we would have more than sufficient instruction from God through Jesus to receive salvation and live a successful Christian life.

He covered everything. We can know God's thoughts on giving to the needy, murder, adultery, retribution, prayer, fasting, worrying, judging others, resting, loving, joy, peace, trust, family, and the end times, just to name a few.

Through Jesus, we see all the attributes of God that were revealed to Moses: compassion, slowness to anger, an abundance of love and faithfulness, and forgiveness. We also see a side of God Moses wasn't shown: His willingness to suffer on our behalf so that we might have fellowship with Him.

Lord Jesus, thank You for revealing the true character of God in Your life and in Your words. . . .

My Thoughts

Seek God Through Music

*"Now write down for yourselves this song and teach it
to the Israelites and have them sing it, so that it
may be a witness for me against them."
(Deut. 31:19)*

I learned my ABCs by learning the little song that is so familiar. Even today when I'm trying to alphabetize something, I find myself humming the song. More and more educators are seeing the value to setting information to music as a way to learn and remember it.

God was actually the first to initiate using the medium of music as a vehicle for teaching. He taught a song to Moses (recorded in Deuteronomy 32) with the purpose of providing the children of Israel with a means to quickly remember God's truths, as well as their forefathers' disobedience.

God created music so that we could be instructed by the words as well as inspired by the music. When I'm having a very difficult day, I find that if I just take ten minutes and either play the keyboard or sing one of my favorite songs, suddenly my spirit is lifted. If you're careful to listen to the music of writers who are diligent Bible students and clearly represent God's truths in their lyrics, you will be blessed and hear God speak through the words and music.

Father, Your words are music to my ears. . . .

My Thoughts

Seek God Through Others

"The Lord sent Nathan to David."
(2 Sam. 12:1)

od used Nathan to speak to David about his sin with Bathsheba. He used Jonah to speak to the sinful people in Nineveh. He used Moses to speak on His behalf to the children of Israel. He used Elijah to speak to the evil Ahab and Jezebel. And He speaks to us through others still.

Many years ago, my husband was offered a position with a successful company. In our decision-making process, he met with our pastor, who advised him that "there is tremendous peace when we are in the center of God's will."

These words stuck with him. Later, Paul made his final visit to the company to take care of last-minute details and pick up his company car—a brand new Cadillac. Then he made the two-hour drive home.

When he walked in the door I thought he had the flu. He was literally green in the face and looked as if he would be sick any moment. He groped his way to the kitchen table and said, "You're not going to understand this, but I can't take this job." Then I sat down. My head felt dizzy. We had no job, no money, and no place to move when our lease was up, and this seemed like an incredible job offer. But I, too, remembered our pastor's words. And it was clear that my husband had absolutely no peace about this. The next day, he returned the car and turned down the offer.

Six months later the company was found guilty of many counts of fraud and dishonesty. Several people in the company were forced to pay huge fines and even serve short jail sentences. Had Paul taken the job, he would have been indicted with the rest.

Lord, help me to heed the godly advice of those You choose to speak to me. . . .

My Thoughts

Seek God in Times of Restlessness

"You will live by the sword and you will serve your brother. But when you grow restless, you will throw his yoke from off your neck."
(Gen. 27:40)

I was visiting with a dear friend of mine, Carole, while in Seattle. As we drove through the beautiful landscape to her house, she shared with me that her spirit was so restless. Having been a pastor's wife for many years, and a very godly woman, she knew that God was speaking to her through this restlessness.

She asked me to pray for her because she sensed that God was leading her in a new direction for her career. This was in November. In January, she was given notice by her company that her position was to be terminated. When the notice was given, she was not angry, resentful, bitter, or even surprised. God's grace had provided a restless spirit so that she and I and others had been in prayer for where God would lead her.

Eventually, another position within the company opened for her—one that she has enjoyed, embraced, and excelled in. She could have ignored this restlessness and brushed it off to hormones, life change, or children marrying and leaving the house! However, prayer about the restlessness prepared her for change in her life—change that would prove positive and refreshing to her.

What if she had ignored the restlessness and not prepared

for God's direction in life? It's possible that she would have been devastated by the news of her position termination. It's possible that she would have internalized hurt and bitterness, which always erupt as anger. Her joy would have been sabotaged. By recognizing and responding to God's restlessness, however, she has experienced inner peace. When handled in prayer, restlessness can trigger restfulness.

Lord, give me rest within the restlessness of my spirit. . . .

My Thoughts

Seek God Through Thanksgiving

*"Do not be anxious about anything, but in everything,
by prayer and petition, with thanksgiving,
present your requests to God."*
(Phil. 4:6)

Many times in the New Testament we read about people praising Jesus and thanking Him *after* He healed them. However, it is a true heart of faith that can thank and praise the Lord *in advance* for the things He will do.

Paul tells us to present our requests to God with thanksgiving. Because we know that every good and perfect thing comes from God and that He longs to give us good gifts, we can thank Him ahead of time for His wondrous answer to our prayers.

A woman recently shared her story of thanksgiving with me that included not only how she had thanked God before her prayer was answered, but also how persistence in prayer had made a difference.

When she and her husband had married almost thirty years ago, neither knew the Lord as their personal Savior. They were good people, striving to be moral and kind, and they gave much back to their community. However, she felt an inexplicable void in her life. While a guest at a Christian Woman's Club luncheon, she quietly gave her life to Christ and became a new creature!

She was so overwhelmed and filled with joy because of her

experience that she rushed home to call her husband at the office to tell him the exciting news. He was less than enthusiastic, understandably, not knowing Christ himself. She began praying that he would also come to be a Christian. Every time she prayed, she prayed by faith and thanked the Lord ahead of time for what He would do in her husband's life.

It took twenty-nine years, but her husband just recently made a commitment to the Lord! She admits that had she not given thanks to the Lord and praised Him each day for what would happen in the future, she would have given up and become very discouraged. Through her thanksgiving, God comforted her.

Lord, my thanks to You overflows! . . .

My Thoughts

Action Steps

So often, God is speaking to us, but we can't hear Him for all the chaos and confusion in our lives. Listening is a very active process. When we are intent on receiving information in a classroom, at a seminar, or during a sermon, we listen attentively, taking notes, keeping ourselves awake. We should listen no less carefully to the Lord.

I believe that there are times when God is very present even when silent. Have you ever spent a day at the beach or gone on a vacation with a close friend? Sometimes there is just such a comfort in being together that no words are necessary. Just to read a book or rest in the presence of the friend is a very peaceful experience. This type of communication is not hard work. Often we can "hear" God's peace just by quietly lingering in His presence.

Here are some ideas for enjoying God's presence.

- Find a quiet spot where you can be alone.
- Try to physically relax. One way to do this is to relax every muscle in your body one by one, beginning with your brow and ending with your toes.
- Empty your mind of your schedule, worries, problems, relationships, and just begin repeating a praise phrase such as "I love You, Lord," or "Praise You Jesus," or "You are worthy."
- Let your mind reflect on Scripture that you've memorized and repeat these verses to yourself.
- Softly sing a praise chorus to the Lord.
- Pray a prayer of praise and thanksgiving.
- Open your mind to what God has to say.
- Rest in His love and presence.

SECTION 8

Introduction Benefits of Prayer

*P*rayer is like exercise—we know we should do it, we know we'd be better off if we did, but somehow we just don't get to it. When we don't exercise, we become sluggish physically. When we don't pray, we get sluggish spiritually. We feel disconnected from God; we're more stressed; worries abound; life feels unfocused and vaguely empty. Not to mention that we don't seem to be handling things as well.

We carry so many burdens in life. God wants to lift those loads, to share their weight and help us to manage them, but He's only able to do that when we pray.

In this section, we're going to remind ourselves of the benefits of prayer. They are nearly endless . . . so prepare to be inspired!

Power When People Pray

He sat between two guards within a prison cell
Awaiting trial and death most certainly
But Peter's godly friends met earnestly in prayer
And as they prayed, an angel set him free!

Chorus

There is power when people pray
For there is power in Jesus' name
Through every trial that we face
All sufficient is God's grace
For there is power, mighty power, when people pray

I too have been enchained
By disappointment, hurt, and pain
So empty was my heart I could not pray
Then in that darkest hour I was reminded of His power
When two or more are gathered in His name!

Bridge

So in those troubled times I've learned to lean on Christian
   friends
And ask them to uplift me through their prayers
Though some trials still remain, somehow I've been
   changed
God's spirit gives me peace, He's always there[1]

Prayer Helps Us Know God

"Teach me your ways so I may know you."
(Ex. 33:13)

For anyone who has read the stories of Moses leading the Isrealites through the wilderness, there is not much question that God answered his prayer positively. In fact, just one chapter later, God describes Himself to Moses as being compassionate, gracious, slow to anger, faithful, loving, and forgiving (34:5-7).

But this familiar description is only the beginning of what Moses came to know of God. Moses' prayer led to a direct answer in the short term, but as he continued to seek out the Lord, his prayer continued to be answered in ways that are less obvious.

When we really want to get to know people, we don't just read their résumés; we spend time talking with them, observing their dealings with us and with other people. The same is true of our relationship with God. The more time we spend talking and listening to Him, the better we will know Him. And the better we know Him, the better we will become at walking in His ways.

Lord, like Moses, I want to know You. Please teach me Your ways. . . .

My Thoughts

Prayer Eases Worry

*"Do not be anxious about anything, but in everything,
by prayer and petition, with thanksgiving,
present your requests to God."*
(Phil. 4:6)

Anxiety plagues our culture like the common cold: it's easy to catch and hard to shake. And sooner or later, everybody has it. We worry about money; we worry about our kids. We fret over our jobs; we're anxious about the future. The list is infinite. In fact, sometimes we even worry about not worrying! At least when we worry, it feels as if we're doing something!

But when we worry, of course, we are actually accomplishing nothing. Nothing good, that is. What worry gains us is increased anxiety—the more we worry, the more we think of to worry about. It also gains us decreased joy, diminished peace, and lack of closeness to God.

Lack of closeness to God? Absolutely. When we are busy worrying, we are *not* busy trusting. Worry doesn't bring God near; it pushes Him away. But if instead we "present our requests to God," we gain something of immeasurable value: "The peace of God, which transcends all understanding, will guard your hearts and your minds in Christ Jesus" (4:7).

Hannah Whitall Smith puts it beautifully:

All through the Old Testament the Lord's one

universal answer to all the fears and anxieties of the children of Israel was the simple words, "I will be with thee." He did not need to say anything more. His presence was to them a perfect guarantee that all their needs would be supplied; and the moment they were assured of it, they were no longer afraid to face the fiercest foe.[2]

Lord, onto Your shoulders I place my worry, and I trust You to care for me. . . .

My Thoughts

Prayer Frees Us from Fear

*"In my anguish I cried to the Lord, and he answered by
setting me free. The Lord is with me; I will not
be afraid. What can man do to me?"*
(Ps. 118:5-6)

When I was a child, my mom kept onions and potatoes in the cool, dark basement. Each evening as she was preparing the meal, she would ask me to run down to the bottom of the stairs and gather up three potatoes and one onion. With every step, it seemed that each little shadow was a big monster lurking in the corners, just waiting to lunge at me and consume me! However, when my dad was working in his shop in the basement, my errand was a joy! I would hop down the stairs and skip over to his workbench for a hug, then get the potatoes and onion for my mom. When Dad was there, I never even noticed any shadows and those monsters mysteriously disappeared! Because Dad was with me, I wasn't afraid.

The only thing we really have to fear is God's wrath when we turn away or are disobedient. As Jesus said, "Do not be afraid of those who kill the body but cannot kill the soul" (Matt. 10:28). Whether we fear events or people or death, God can give us courage. After all, even if someone were to take our physical body from us, he cannot take our soul. If our soul is committed to God the Father, we truly have nothing to fear!

Thank You, Father, for walking with me through the valley of the shadow of my fears. . . .

My Thoughts

Prayer Brings Inner Peace

*"Peace I leave with you; my peace I give you. I do not
give to you as the world gives. Do not let your
hearts be troubled and do not be afraid."
(John 14:27)*

*I*n this verse from John's Gospel, Jesus is just winding
up some teaching about a Counselor, the Holy Spirit,
who would be coming to comfort His disciples after His
ascension to heaven—and that same Holy Spirit has been available to all believers ever since. The Holy Spirit actually dwells
within us, offering us this remarkable inner peace. Peace is more
than just the absence of conflict. Peace is a calmness, a quiet
tranquillity.

While teaching a Sunday School lesson one time, my husband placed a glass of water in a volunteer's hand; then he
shook the volunteer's arm. Of course, water spilled everywhere.
He asked the class why, and the answer was obvious—he had
shaken the guy's arm! The point he was making was that when
we are shaken, whatever is inside us spills out. If we are filled
with anger or bitterness, these are the things we spill over. If we
are filled with anxiety, that is what will come out. However,
when we are filled with God's peace, hostility is replaced by
unity, confusion is replaced by order, division is replaced by har-
mony, anger is replaced by joy.

As Jesus reminded us, He offers us a peace that the world
does not and cannot give. Advertisers lead us to believe that we

will enjoy peace when we make a certain amount of money, take a certain exotic vacation, buy a certain car, and wear a certain brand of clothing.

The truth is that no matter where we are or what our circumstances, our inner self accompanies us everywhere. No amount of traveling or dressing up our outward appearance can change what is on the inside—only God can do that. And He can only do that if we ask Him to through prayer

Lord, please help me to be so filled with Your inner peace that I spill peace to everyone I meet. . . .

My Thoughts

Prayer Helps Us Obtain Insight and Understanding

"While I was speaking and praying, confessing my sin and the sin of my people Israel and making my request to the Lord my God for his holy hill—while I was still in prayer, Gabriel, the man I had seen in the earlier vision, came to me in swift flight about the time of the evening sacrifice. He instructed me and said to me, 'Daniel, I have now come to give you insight and understanding.'"
(Dan. 9:20-22)

For Daniel, prayer and speaking with God lead to insight and understanding. They can for us as well.

Insight is the ability to grasp intuitively the essence of a situation. It involves discernment, or acuteness of judgment, and perception, which is an immediate recognition. *Understanding* is being able to know and interpret God's ways. It is important to note that it was because prayer was a part of Daniel's daily routine that he was given insight and understanding. He consistently walked closely with God and sought His heart, making sure to confess his sins.

Although it would be spectacular to actually see and hear from an angel, we no longer have need of this kind of messenger. The Holy Spirit within us reveals God's message to us and gives us insight and understanding. We only need to pray for it.

Lord, please take the scales from my eyes so that I can see and understand Your message. . . .

My Thoughts

Prayer Leads to Good Decisions

"Fashion a breastpiece for making decisions."
(Ex. 28:15)

Moses' brother, Aaron, was given the responsibility of being the first high priest for the nation of Israel. After him, the position of high priest was to be handed down to the first son of every generation. Although a hereditary position, the high priest was expected to exemplify through character and conduct a purity and dependence upon God, because it was through the high priest that sinful man gained access to a holy God.

The priestly garments that God instructed Aaron to construct represented the high priest's function as mediator between God and man. The ephod was a two- piece apron that featured on its front two onyx stones bearing the names of the twelve tribes of Israel. Attached to this was the "breastplate of judgment" with twelve precious stones engraved with the names of the twelve tribes.

God commanded that there be a pocket sown onto this apron directly over the high priest's heart; in this pocket, Urim and Thummim were to be kept. These are thought to have been two items, the Urim representing curses and Thummim representing "yes" or "no" answers. These would be drawn out by the priest as the way to discover God's decisions.

If only it were that simple today! Wouldn't it be great to

draw out a "yes" or "no" card from a pocket and know what decision to make! But now, we don't need a priest to access God for us. Since Jesus acts now as our High Priest, He is the one we can call upon to help us discern God's will for our lives. Through prayer, we can make our requests known and hear His answer.

Lord God, please help me to hear in my heart the good decisions You want me to make. . . .

My Thoughts

Prayer Helps Us Walk with the Spirit

"Let us keep in step with the Spirit."
(Gal. 5:25)

During the American Revolution, opposing armies came together in a field, marching in step by the beat of the drum. The beat would slow when not in battle, keeping the troops together, and would quicken as they marched to meet their adversary. If anyone were to fall out of step, it could cause many men to trip and fall.

Our adversary is the Devil. He is on a seek-and- destroy mission to obliterate us, spiritually speaking. Therefore, we must keep in step with the Spirit so that we are unified with Him in battle. Prayer is one of the things that keeps us aligned with Him, along with Bible study and worship and fellowship. If we lag behind the step of the Spirit, we begin to lose our focus on God's goodness. We also lose the confidence that we find in Him and the power that He gives to us. If we sprint ahead of the Spirit, we tend to become prideful, thinking we can fight the battle on our own.

However, if we keep in step with the Spirit, we will enjoy the fruits of the Spirit: love, joy, peace, patience, kindness, goodness, faithfulness, gentleness, and self-control (Gal. 5:22, 23). Staying side-by-side with Him also ensures God's direction and protection and keeps us in pace with His plan.

Lord, please keep me in step with Your Spirit. . . .

My Thoughts

Prayer Enables Us to Enjoy Friendship with God

"The Lord would speak to Moses face to face,
as a man speaks with his friend."
(Ex. 33:11)

God created in all of us a yearning for fellowship with others and with Him. Yet not all of us recognize our desire to be friends with God, and not all of us attain that friendship.

What was it about Moses that caused God to develop such a special friendship with him? Look at Moses' past—he was far from perfect. He was a murderer (Ex. 2:12), he was a coward (v. 15), he was disobedient (4:13), and he had a terrible temper (32:19). Yet no matter what Moses did, God kept responding to him.

Genesis 1:26 says that God created man in His own image. Can we assume, then, that God desires fellowship with us as much as we desire it with Him? Even though He knows our every thought, He has filled His Word with instructions for us to pray. Can it be partly because He wants to hear our voice, to talk with us, keep us company, be our Friend?

We can learn about God in the Bible. But we can only befriend God through prayer.

Father God, thank You for befriending us! . . .

181

My Thoughts

Prayer Can Give Us Divine Direction

⁓⁓

"Then they prayed, 'Lord, you know everyone's heart.
Show us which of these two you have chosen.'"
(Acts 1:24)

After Christ ascended into heaven, His disciples were left behind, waiting for the power of the Holy Spirit to come upon them. Before Christ's ascension, this small band of men had always been called disciples, which means *learners*. After he ascended, they were known as apostles, which means *those sent on a mission*. Being sent on a mission requires extensive preparation and a clear goal. Their time with Christ had prepared them to go out and share this Good News with the world.

Since Judas had betrayed Jesus and then committed suicide, the men were looking for a replacement. Two men became valid candidates for this position, so the apostles went to the Lord in prayer asking Him to show them which of the two God had chosen for this job.

It's interesting that they ended up drawing lots as a way for God to reveal to them His choice; a man named Matthias won. However, shortly after this, the Holy Spirit came upon them This is the last time the Bible records the casting of lots as a means of discerning God's will.

Because of the presence of the Holy Spirit, we now have a direct connection to God the Father. The Holy Spirit reveals God's will directly to us. He uses many different means to make

His revelation to us: godly counsel; biblical principles; that still, small voice that can't be quieted; lack or presence of peace. But often, He makes it known to us while we are in prayer.

Lord, I want to seek You at every turn of my life. Thank You for Your divine direction. . . .

My Thoughts

Prayer Leads to Joy

"Ask and you will receive, and your joy will be complete."
(John 16:24)

What could possibly be better than "complete" joy? All of us can think of things that we're pretty sure would make us feel complete joy. Losing weight. Having a new house. An unexpected raise. But are these the things this verse says to ask for?

This is a passage many of us are uncomfortable with. Obviously, there have been many things we have asked for but have not received—yet this appears to be a clear-cut promise.

John F. Walvoord and Roy B. Zuck offer insight into what this verse is really saying . . . and as they do, we catch a glimpse of what truly brings us joy, as opposed to what we think will bring us joy. In this passage in the Gospel of John, Jesus is talking to His disciples not too long before His death. He is trying to explain how things will be different after He is gone.

> The forthcoming events brought about changed
> relations. . . . [The disciples] would be His ambassa-
> dors and therefore had the right to ask the Father
> for whatever they needed to accomplish His will.
> The words "in my name" are not a magical formula
> which enable the user to get *his* will done; instead
> those words tied the requests to the work of the Son
> in doing the *Father's* will.[3]

The disciples could not fathom having any joy at all without Jesus' physical presence (John 16:17-22). But Jesus' physical presence with them would very soon not be part of God's will. Verses 22-33 are intended to comfort the disciples and to give them hope that they would once again experience joy, even without the Person they loved the most.

When we ask the Father for what we need in order to do His will, we can be sure we will receive it. And despite what we often think to the contrary, doing the Father's will is what brings us the greatest joy.

Lord, thank You for joy that lives deep in my heart. . . .

My Thoughts

Prayer Results in Good Gifts

*"If you, then, though you are evil, know how to give
good gifts to your children, how much more will your
Father in heaven give good gifts to those who ask him."*
(Matt. 7:11)

In the Old Testament, most of the references to gifts
involve man giving gifts to God, either as a sacrifice, a
plea for forgiveness, or as a request for a favor. In the
New Testament, the prevalent theme is of God offering gifts to
man.

What kinds of gifts does God offer us? Here are some, for
starters.

1. *Salvation.* Through Jesus Christ we have been redeemed
   or saved from the penalty of sin. "For it is by grace you
   have been saved, through faith—and this not from yourselves, it is the gift of God" (Eph. 2:8).

2. *Eternal Life.* Salvation guarantees us life after death. "For
   the wages of sin is death, but the gift of God is eternal life
   in Christ Jesus our Lord" (Rom. 6:23).

3. *Necessities of Life.* God meets our basic needs. "Give us
   today our daily bread" (Matt. 6:11).

4. *The Holy Spirit.* Jesus sends His Comforter to us. "And
   you will receive the gift of the Holy Spirit" (Acts 2:38).

5. *Spiritual Abilities.* We enjoy supernatural abilities as a
   result of our relationship with God. "There are different

kinds of gifts, but the same Spirit" (1 Cor. 12:4).

Lord, I ask for and accept the gifts that You have chosen just for me! . . .

My Thoughts

Prayer Brings Us Rest

*"Come to me, all you who are weary and burdened,
and I will give you rest."*
(Matt. 11:28)

*I*t's easy to get so busy serving God (and our families, friends, relatives, coworkers)—feeling so burdened by the needs around us—that we forget one of the first seven things God initiated on earth. After spending six days creating the world, He rested on the seventh—and declared that we should too. In this passage from Matthew, the word *rest* comes from the Greek word *anapauo*, which means *calm, comfort, and refreshment*. Doesn't that sound good right now? In a world that is in constant turmoil, what a blessing to have access to rest! Isaiah 57:20-22 reminds us that "the wicked are like the tossing sea, which cannot rest. . . . There is no peace . . . for the wicked." But for us, calm, comfort, and refreshment are always only a prayer away.

Praying keeps us calm, like the stillness in the eye of a storm. Praying comforts us, reminding us of God's goodness and His availability to us in times of trouble. Praying refreshes us, giving us renewed energy and strength. As Isaiah tells us:

> Those who hope in the Lord will renew their strength.
> They will soar on wings like eagles;
> they will run and not grow weary,
> they will walk and not be faint (40:31).

Lord, thank You for the calm, comfort, and refreshment you offer. . . .

My Thoughts

Prayer Unifies Us

⁕

"They all joined together constantly in prayer, along with the women and Mary the mother of Jesus, and with his brothers."
(Acts 1:14)

Could there possibly have been a more unified group than the disciples after Jesus' ascension? Before the coming of the Holy Spirit, they were pretty much a ragtag bunch, largely uncomprehending of what Jesus was up to, squabbling among themselves. But afterward—you'd hardly recognize them! In the Gospels, we catch glimpses of tiffs and minor jealousies among them. But in Acts, there is none of that. They present a strong, cohesive, unified front to new converts, to dissenters, and to opposition alike.

No doubt the presence of the Holy Spirit had a lot to do with this change. But there's no escaping the fact that prayer was a factor too. Remember Jesus' prayer for them in John 17, just before His death? His overriding request was that they would be "one." And it must be more than a coincidence that in this record of astonishing acts on the part of the disciples, the very first chapter tells us that they "joined together constantly in prayer."

Praying together, even if you're not specifically praying for unity, can't help but create unity. Have you ever tried praying with someone you're mad at, for instance? It's almost impossible. Either you'll get the anger over with first, or you'll be finished with it by the time you're done praying, generally speaking. Sin just can't stand up in the presence of the Lord. And coming before Him jointly unites us in our common love for Him, making all other issues fade in their significance.

Lord, thank You for the privilege of uniting in Your name. . . .

My Thoughts

Prayer Leads to Provision

"Give us today our daily bread."
(Matt. 6:11)

The simplest and most familiar of Bible prayers—one that is recorded for us as a pattern for our own prayers—reassures us that God is interested in our daily physical needs as well as our spiritual ones. In fact, it is sometimes through His meeting of these down-to-earth basic needs that we are most aware of His presence.

Several years ago, my family traveled a painful financial road as a result of extended unemployment. Here was my husband, a good-looking, articulate, well-educated, and well-networked individual who could not find employment. For more than four years we struggled to find adequate work to bring in enough to cover our basic needs.

But during this time, God's faithfulness became so real to us. A hundred-dollar bill was placed in my hand several times after church; a thousand-dollar check was given to us from a godly couple; groceries were literally left on our doorstep; beautiful name-brand clothing was handed over to us by caring friends. These gifts always arrived just at the time of need and often became an abundant over-supply!

God has not forgotten you. He sees what you need, and if you ask, He will supply it.

Father, thank You for clothing me more beautifully than the lilies and feeding me the Bread of Life. . . .

My Thoughts

Action Steps

What benefits of prayer have you experienced, either during the reading of this book or at other times in your life? Describe them here, and receive the encouragement of those benefits all over again.

- Can you remember a time (or times) when you were anxious or worried about a situation and God gave you peace?

- What decisions has God helped you to make that have proved successful for you?

- What have you learned about God's character through your prayer time with Him?

- How have you seen God provide for your needs? Be specific.

- In what ways has unity with other believers been the result of prayer?

- In what other ways have you been blessed through prayer?

Conclusion

*J*esus Christ.
His power formed the very foundations of our universe at Creation. His death on the cross brings forgiveness to our sins. His gift of the Holy Spirit now comforts and abides within us. It is because of His Resurrection that we are assured of eternal life. His gift of the Holy Spirit now comforts and abides within us. It is through Jesus that our prayers are heard. And He continues to pray on our behalf to God the Father.

"What a privilege to carry everything to God in prayer."

By His Wounds

By His wounds we are healed
Through His blood the pardon sealed
Through His Word truth revealed
That can save and set us free

Jesus washed away each stain
The precious Lamb of God was slain

By His death we now live
Through His mighty power to forgive

Jesus takes away our sin
And gives new life within[1]

Bibliography

Bounds, E. M., *The Complete Works of E. M. Bounds on Prayer,* Baker Book House, Grand Rapids, Mich., 1990.

Chambers, Oswald, *If You Will Ask,* Discovery House Publishers, Grand Rapids, Mich., 1985.

Complete Bible Commentary (The), Thomas Nelson Publishers, Nashville, Tenn., 1999.

Henry, Matthew, *Commentary on the Whole Bible,* Hendrickson Publishers, Peabody, Mass., 1998.

Illustrated Bible Handbook, Thomas Nelson Publishers, Nashville, Tenn., 1997.

Keller, Phillip, *Elijah: Prophet of Power,* WordBooks, Waco, Texas, 1980.

Knoll, Woodrow Kroll, *Empowered to Pray,* Baker Books, Grand Rapids, Mich. 1995.

Liberty Illustrated Bible Dictionary (The), Thomas Nelson Publishers, Nashville, Tenn., 1986.

Life Application Study Bible, Tyndale House Publishers, Wheaton, Ill., 1996.

New International Encyclopedia of Bible Words, Zondervan Publishing House, Grand Rapids, Mich. 1991.

Payne, Leanne, *Listening Prayer,* Baker Book House, Grand Rapids, Mich., 1994.

Rice, John R., *Prayer: Asking and Receiving,* Sword of the Lord Publishers, Murfreesboro, Tenn., 1942.

Sailhamer, John H., *NIV Compact Bible Commentary*, Zondervan Publishing, Grand Rapids, Mich., 1994.

Smith, Gordon T., *Listening to God in Times of Choice*, InterVarsity Press, Downers Grove, Ill., 1997.

Stanley, Charles, *How to Listen to God*, Thomas Nelson Publishers, Nashville, Tenn., 1985

Stanley, Charles, *Talking with God*, Thomas Nelson Publishers, Nashville, Tenn., 1997.

Vine, W.E., *Vine's Expository Dictionary of New Testament Words*, out of print.

Endnotes

One
1. Richard J. Foster, *Celebration of Discipline* (San Francisco: Harper & Row Publishers, 1978), p. 30.
2. Julie Baker, "The Resting Place" as recorded on *I Can Do All Things* (1987).
3. See W. E. Vine, F. F. Bruce, ed., *Vine's Expository Dictionary of Old and New Testament Words* (Old Tappan, N.J.: Fleming H. Revell Co., 1981), p. 207.

Two
1. Foster, *Celebration of Discipline*, pp. 33, 31.
2. Julie Baker, "Open Hands" as recorded on *Faithful* (1997).
3. Merrill F. Unger, *Unger's Bible Dictionary* (Chicago, Ill.: Moody Press, 1973), p. 927.
4. Foster, p. 33.

Three
1 Julie Baker, "Up to the Mountain" as recorded on *I Can Do All Things* (1997).
2.Foster, *Celebration of Discipline*, p. 36.

Four
1. Julie Baker, "When We Pray" as recorded on *Take Time to Sing* (1998).
2. See John F. Walvoord and Roy B. Zuck, *The Bible Knowledge Commentary*, New Testament edition (Wheaton, Ill.: Victor Books, 1983), p. 399.
3. Walvoord and Zuck, p. 399.

Five
1. Julie Baker, "He Is Faithful" as recorded on *Faithful* (1997).
2. Walvoord and Zuck, *The Bible Knowledge Commentary*, New Testament ed., p. 668.
3. John F. Walvoord and Roy B. Zuck, *The Bible Knowledge Commentary*,

Old Testament ed. (Wheaton, Ill.: Victor Books, 1985), p. 961.

Six

1. Julie Baker, "The Father Cares for You" as recorded on *Because We're Sisters* (1999).
2. See Walvoord and Zuck, *The Bible Knowledge Commentary*, New Testament ed., p. 829.

Seven

1. Julie Baker, "Take Time to Pray" as recorded on *Faithful* (1997).
2. Foster, *Celebration of Discipline*, p.27.
3. As quoted in Foster, p. 18.

Eight

1. Julie Baker, "Power When People Pray" as recorded on *Attitude of Prayer* (1993).
2. Hannah Whitall Smith, *The God of All Comfort* (Westwood, N.J.: The Christian Library, 1984), p. 73.
3. Walvoord and Zuck, *The Bible Knowledge Commentary*, New Testament ed., p. 329.

Conclusion

1. Julie Baker, "By His Wounds" as recorded on *Take Time to Sing* (1998).